MEANING

HOW LEADERS CREATE MEANING AND CLARITY DURING TIMES OF CRISIS AND OPPORTUNITY

Brian!

Here is to more success in leadership and seeing others success as a result.

ASH SEDDEEK AND LESLIE A. RUBIN

July 2019

ACKNOWLEDGMENTS

Special thanks to Dr. Ossama Hassanein for believing in the cause of this book and the leadership communication lessons it will provide to current and future leaders. Thanks also to my co-author, Leslie Rubin, for crystalizing the importance of the book and its target audience, and then joining me on this journey, which made us better communicators with more empathy for leaders everywhere.

— Ash Seddeek

I'm so glad I picked up the phone the day Ash called to invite me on this journey. I'm grateful to have you as a friend and co-author. We could not have done this project without our book coach, Bonnie Budzowski, and her expert guidance during this project.

— Leslie A. Rubin

CONTENTS

FOREWORD

Whether it's a market transition, a crisis or opportunity, the ability of a leader to communicate is often the difference between success and failure. In our ever changing, fast-paced world, leaders need everyone to be engaged, aligned, and performing at their best. Leaders must be more open and transparent than ever before, creating environments of inclusivity versus ones of command and control. A winning culture includes a set of values and behaviors that the entire organization uses as the North Star.

In a quest to uncover how successful leaders do this in practice, especially in times of crisis or opportunity, Ash Seddeek and Leslie Rubin created a powerhouse of a book. They interviewed 12 amazing leaders, asking each to describe a real-world example of exactly how they engaged and guided a team or organization through an especially intense time—either to navigate through a crisis or capture an opportunity.

The result is 12 in-depth case studies of exceptional leadership performance that span various industries spread across the globe. You'll read about startups, corporations with long histories, and nonprofits. Chances are you'll learn something new about the challenges and opportunities in the manufacturing, services, medical device, and driverless car industries, as well as how to transform a university. Equally important, you'll learn about executive learning curves and missteps. The leadership behaviors you'll discover can be applied immediately.

In chapters culled from interviews, Ash and Leslie share the experiences of these leaders, harnessing the power of experiences which tested their leadership mettle and challenged the survival of their organizations. Each chapter reveals how a leader used continuous and consistent communications to pull through and take the crisis or opportunity by the horns.

As a global "culture and talent" expert and author of *More than Casual Fridays* and *Free Coffee: Building a Business Culture that Works for Everyone*, my goal is to help people and companies recognize how to engage and energize their teams, develop creative "culture and talent" strategies to meet changing market requirements, and build high-performing, values-based cultures. Working with CEOs such as John Chambers of Cisco, Glen Tullman of Allscripts, Lars Björk of Qlik, and David Levin at McGraw-Hill, gave me an opportunities to see great leaders and communicators up close and personal. These leaders and the leaders you will meet in this book were strategic in their leadership communication efforts, and it ultimately transformed their companies and careers.

That's why I am so excited about this book. Communications and culture are so closely intertwined that it's hard to separate them. Working my way through the 12 leadership behaviors that Ash and Leslie identified as common to all of the success stories, I kept saying, "Yes, yes, yes!" The core and primary lesson in this book is to communicate, communicate, and communicate. This can't be emphasized enough.

Don't miss this book—whether you are a veteran CEO, a leader on the rise, someone who wants to know what it takes to manage better in your organization, or someone who desires to be a more effective communicator—there is something here for you.

Enjoy!

— Diane K. Adams

CHAPTER 1

INTRODUCTION

In March 2000, at the peak of the dot-com boom, Cisco became the most valuable company in the world. Its market cap reached a staggering $555.4 billion, and the company surpassed Microsoft in value.

Fast forward to the years between 2008 and 2011, and things were radically different. Of course, Cisco, like all companies, had struggled at various times throughout its history, but not like this. At that time, CEO John Chambers told *TheStreet.com*, "The company has survived tough times before, but its current plight is radically different than the dot-com bust."

We had the privilege of working with Cisco's top 200 executives, and we saw them in action, particularly as they handled existential threats during the 2008 financial crisis. This crisis was compounded by technology trends that were going to render Cisco irrelevant. All this after Cisco had become synonymous with the rise of the Internet in the 2000s.

Our experience at Cisco during that economic downturn is one of the factors that led us to a deep study of leadership communications, especially during times of crisis and opportunity.

Leslie Rubin had several roles at Cisco, which involved supporting the executive and strategic communications of senior executives. Leslie led the executive communications team for the Office of the Chairman and CEO under John Chambers, and then later managed the executive communications individuals working closely with the Cisco executive leadership team and operating committee.

Ash Seddeek served as a content strategy manager for Cisco's largest events, such as the Global Sales Experience and Partner Summit. In this role, he saw many Cisco leaders face internal and external challenges. His role was to understand the company's external dynamic challenges, market positioning, and business priorities, and then to work with the top 200 leaders in how to communicate the way forward by clearly articulating the what, how, and why—particularly "why Cisco and why now."

Ash had a close-up view of the value and practice of organizational communications as delivered by these senior leaders. He saw how the executive messages helped bring clarity, sustain business momentum, and retain top talent. Ash worked with Leslie and scores of executive communications managers at Cisco around the globe to align and stay on message. He then worked with these executives over full-year cycles to evolve the messaging, create their various communications, and deliver them with conviction.

Ash now runs a management consulting company focused on sales and leadership for Fortune 500 companies. He is the founder of Top 1% Sellers Academy and the Top 1% Sellers Podcast on iTunes and C-Suite Radio. He has also integrated his experience with top leaders and sellers into a success formula called the *Own It Win It Crush It* formula for peak performance. Ash published this success formula in a best-selling book with Jack Canfield, *Road to Success.*

Leslie now runs her own global executive strategy and communications consulting company. Her clients are C-level executives who rely on her to develop and coach them on building their brand for maximum impact. She also works with executive teams on elevating their communication dynamics to drive business results.

In addition to their individual companies, Ash and Leslie are co-founders of the Executive Greatness Institute (EGI). EGI is a leadership communications company offering services to help business leaders create a strong leadership brand, executive presence, and a solid messaging platform. Ash and Leslie pride themselves on helping leaders hone their communications skills by working with a dream team of executive coaches and experts.

HOW WE DUG DEEPLY INTO LEADERSHIP COMMUNICATION: OUR STUDY

Our experiences at Cisco and other organizations sparked a deep interest in how leaders create meaning and clarity. We've seen first-hand how important it is for executives to communicate in ways that not only inform but motivate and inspire the organization, its partners, and the markets on the company's vision, competitive positioning, and differentiation.

Leaders develop a unique level of comfort with ambiguity and uncertainty because that's part of being a good leader. This makes it easy for them to forget that ambiguity and uncertainty are difficult conditions for employees or stakeholders.

Ron Ricci, Vice President at Cisco, and co-author of *The Collaboration Imperative,* says:

> *Leaders must understand that decisions are like best-selling novels; the greater the ambiguity around a decision, the faster it moves up the* New York Times *bestseller list. People's natural curiosities and ambiguity seem to feed on each other. In worst cases, ambiguity leads to conspiracy theories and people work against each other. In most cases, work simply slows down while people seek out answers.*
>
> *... There's more than enough evidence to demonstrate that teams produce higher results when they can align their individual work to the greater mission and strategy*

of the organization. When all goes right, organizations can produce discretionary effort—that amazing, hard-to-bottle effort people give when ambiguity is replaced by a sense of shared purpose.

In times of uncertainty, employees want to know the answers to fundamental questions: What does everything that is happening mean for the company? What does it mean for our customers and partners? More importantly, what does it mean to each one of us at an individual level? What will the impact of these challenges be, particularly on our jobs and the stability for us today and going forward?

Regarding clarity, employees want to know answers to these questions: Given what's happening, how are we going to handle the present? How do we chart a path to our future? What risks are we facing? What promises can leaders make with certainty, and what promises can they make with caveats?

We decided to seek out respected leaders in a variety of organizations and industries to see what we could learn from their experiences and perspectives. How had top leaders dealt with intense organizational challenges, whether at times of crisis or opportunity? How had they applied their leadership communications across all stakeholders?

We wanted to see how leaders responded in high stakes situations and then share what we learned with our clients—and you. We wanted to identify the key leadership qualities, behaviors, and communication cadence leaders apply to lead their organizations out of a crisis or into compelling high-value opportunities.

How We Dug Deeply into
Leadership Communication: Our Participants

We sought out successful leaders from diverse situations and conducted structured interviews to ensure we got comparable information from each. Participants represented CEOs, CIOs, inventors, startup visionaries, investors, a coaching executive, and a president of a university. Here is a brief description of each participant.

1. SHEILA JORDAN
   SVP AND CIO OF SYMANTEC CORPORATION
   Jordan was charged with creating an internal IT organization to support Symantec. This task wasn't even complete when her team was given 12 months to structure and rally Symantec's IT organization to split away from Veritas and create a full-fledged IT infrastructure to support Symantec.

2. DR. NIDO QUBEIN
   PRESIDENT OF HIGH POINT UNIVERSITY
   An accomplished business leader and dedicated philanthropist, Qubein took the helm of an obscure school in 2005. Qubein led the university through an extraordinary transformation, including major increases in traditional undergraduate enrollment (from 1,450 to 4,500 students), the number of faculty (from 108 to 300), and the addition of 90 new and acquired buildings on campus, with a total investment of one billion dollars.

3. DR. PRITH BANERJEE
   EVP AND CTO OF SCHNEIDER ELECTRIC
   When Prith Banerjee joined Schneider Electric with a mandate for change from the CEO, he was the very definition of an outsider. From a different culture, ethnicity, and industry, Banerjee traveled around the globe building a leadership coalition around renewed innovation throughout the organization.

4. HALA FADEL
   CO-FOUNDER AND
   MANAGING PARTNER OF LEAP VENTURES
   Fadel started her career in 1996 at Merrill Lynch in mergers and acquisitions and now leads a venture capital firm

based in Beirut and Dubai. She is the founder and chair of
the MIT Enterprise Forum of the Pan-Arab Region, an organization that promotes entrepreneurship and organizes,
among other things, the MIT Arab startup competition.

5.   RANA EL KALIOUBY
     CO-FOUNDER AND CEO OF AFFECTIVA
     el Kaliouby, a pioneer in facial expression recognition re-
     search and technology development, pursued an academic
     career—until she realized that creating a startup would
     make a bigger impact in the world. When the resulting
     company was veering off course from its original vision,
     she led the charge to get the company back on track.

6.   DR. OSSAMA HASSANEIN
     CHAIRMAN OF RISING TIDE FUND. ENTREPRENEUR,
     MENTOR, AND VENTURE CAPITALIST
     Hassanein has managed over $1 billion of international
     technology funds in diverse leadership roles, including
     those of EVP of Berkeley International in San Francisco,
     Chairman of Technocom Ventures in Paris, President of
     Newbridge Networks Holdings in Canada, and Senior
     Managing Director of Newbury Ventures.

7.   RAJ PURI
     CEO OF YANNA TECHNOLOGIES
     Puri is a technologist and an entrepreneur with a unique
     blend of technical and business acumen. He has 25-plus
     years of diverse professional experience, spanning from
     starting new ventures and creating new products and ser-
     vices, to evangelizing unique business models, to launch-
     ing new international markets. Puri has specialized expe-
     rience in cybersecurity and compliance matters with busi-
     ness engagements in the United States, Europe, and Asia.

8.   DAVID MARTIN
     CEO OF CARDIOVASCULAR SYSTEMS INC.
     Martin led the business through a major expansion into
     the coronary artery disease market, a longtime goal of the

company's founders. During Martin's tenure, CSI grew from a pre-revenue, startup organization to a public company with fiscal year 2015 revenues in excess of $180 million with two unique, high-margin applications addressing vascular disease.

9. SUZANNE EVANS
   FOUNDER AND OWNER OF SUZANNE EVANS
   COACHING, LLC
   When Evans started her business, she went from secretary to surpassing the seven-figure mark in just over three years. Today, she supports, coaches, and teaches over 30,000 women enrolled in her wealth and business building programs. Evans has become the "Tell it like it is," no fluff boss of business building.

10. DR. LOUAY ELDADA
    CO-FOUNDER AND CEO OF QUANERGY SYSTEMS, INC.
    Eldada is a serial entrepreneur, having founded and sold three businesses to Fortune 100 companies. Quanergy is his fourth startup. Eldada is a technical business leader with a proven record of accomplishment at both small and large companies. With 70 patents, he is a recognized expert in nanotechnology, photonic integrated circuits, and advanced optoelectronics.

11. VINCE PIZZICA
    SEVP OF TECHNICOLOR
    In late 2008, Pizzica and Frederick Rose joined a French company called Thompson SA, expecting to revitalize the historic global company. With the economic downturn, the company lost an investor to the tune of half a billion dollars. Today the company, rebranded as Technicolor, is on strong footing again. It took two years to guide the company's emergence from the French bankruptcy process, generate cash flow, and rebuild the balance sheet to the point at which it could start making acquisitions.

12. Dr. Rosina L. Racioppi
    President and CEO of WOMEN Unlimited Inc.
Racioppi spearheads her organization's initiatives to help
Fortune 1000 companies cultivate the talent they need for
ongoing growth and profitability. Under her leadership,
WOMEN Unlimited, Inc. successfully partners with organizations across a wide range of industries to develop
their high-potential women and to build a pipeline of diverse and talented leaders.

How We Dug Deeply into Leadership Communication: Our Interview Structure

Our interview questions were designed in four parts to help us
uncover each leader's leadership communication philosophy.

Part 1 focused on the leadership event or challenge the
participants chose to share with us. The questions were designed to uncover the context as well as the story. We wanted
to explore a key event in their leadership journey, whether that
event was an opportunity or a crisis.

Part 2 was structured to uncover the participants' initial
thought processes as they started to address the crisis or opportunity. We asked questions about their leadership communications. What were their first steps? How did they assess
their situation?

In Part 3, we sought to learn participants' response strategies. What did they decide to do? With whom did they collaborate, inside and outside of the organization? From whom did
they seek help? What methods did they use to distribute key
messages and allay fears? Our intent here was to uncover how
these leaders handled the leadership challenge and how they
engaged the larger organization.

In Part 4, we focused on leadership reflections. We wanted to get to know the human being behind each one of the stories. We were interested in hearing the leaders' own reflections on how they felt during the overall experience and how it

helped them grow as individuals as well as leaders. We asked about their inspiration and mentors as well as any advice they would offer emerging leaders.

We dedicated a chapter to each of the participants interviewed. As you read the chapters and hear from CEOs and executives in large and small companies, you'll see that their challenges have common elements. The differences come in how a leader takes charge, acting responsibly, authentically, and in a timely manner with all parties concerned.

Each participant had the choice of sharing an opportunity or crisis with us. In either situation, leadership communication is a "must" rather than a "nice-to-have" option.

HOW WE DUG DEEPLY INTO
LEADERSHIP COMMUNICATION: OUR RESULTS

The 12 executives we interviewed shared their stories, strategies, and lessons learned with us. We are grateful for their transparency as well as their eagerness to help. Although each situation and the personality of each leader is different, common themes and behaviors repeated themselves throughout the interviews. After careful analysis of the interviews, we identified 10 leadership behaviors that produce meaning and clarity.

The first five behaviors have to do with the leaders themselves. These behaviors provide a sense of grounding that allows the leaders to remain calm and clearheaded in the face of challenge or opportunity. An effective leader has a measure of fortitude and a network of support in place before major change or uncertainty strikes.

The second five behaviors focus on followers and other stakeholders. These are the communication behaviors that provide clarity and meaning in the face of uncertainty.

Some of the behaviors we identified aren't all that surprising. For example, you won't be surprised to learn that a leader must clarify the vision of the organization. On the other hand, you might not expect that an effective leader must cultivate authentic humility. And when you consider the 10 behaviors as integrated, each building on the other, you have a fresh challenge. The following chapters demonstrate how these behaviors work, with ingenuity and integrity, in real and diverse situations. You'll find the accounts both interesting and illustrative.

Here are the 10 leadership behaviors that lead to clarity and meaning:

1. ACCEPT THE REALITY THAT
    BUSINESS CYCLES INEVITABLY EBB AND FLOW
    As each leader chose his or her own crisis or opportunity to highlight in this book, the timetables for events vary. In some chapters, you'll read about leaders who were in growth phases or introducing strategic change. In these instances, the leader was concerned about sustainability as business cycles inevitably change. In other chapters, you'll read about organizations that were dramatically affected by the economic crisis between the years of 2008 to 2011. The leaders in those circumstances didn't panic. Rather, they carefully assessed their situations and created a strategy to fit reality. In either case, the leader trusted that the business cycle would eventually change. That belief allowed the leader to cultivate and communicate patience, perseverance, and confidence.

2. CULTIVATE THE HABITS OF LISTENING AND LEARNING
    University president Nido Qubein teaches students that leadership and followership are partners. "If you hope to be an effective leader, you must also be a lifetime learner, a lifetime student. This means that you are being coached as well as coaching others. You are following your own heroes, models, and mentors."

    Vince Pizzica of Technicolor shares Qubein's commitment to learning. Early in his career, as the youngest technology executive at Telstra, Pizzica actively sought out external mentors, many of whom were CEOs of companies in the industry or even adjacent companies. Recently, he has begun to look again for external mentors, with a focus on the industry level in the San Francisco Bay Area.

3. CULTIVATE AUTHENTIC HUMILITY
Leaders who build the most effective teams are the ones who have accepted their own limitations and come to appreciate the strengths of those around them. A commitment to lifelong learning is one demonstration of this humility. Another is the willingness to pitch in at whatever level your team is working.

Coaching guru Suzanne Evans remembers a basketball coach who told team members, "I will never ask you to run a suicide run that I wouldn't run." In similar manner, Evans says, "If there is a stain on the carpet and everyone is struggling, I'll be one of the first ones to get down and take a turn."

4. CLARIFY AND FOCUS ON THE
ORGANIZATION'S MISSION AND VALUES
The leader is the keeper of the organization's purpose. Without a shared purpose and values, employees won't have the loyalty, alignment, or energy the organization needs to succeed. You'll find evidence of this leadership commitment to mission and values repeatedly throughout the chapters.

For example, Raj Puri interviews every employee who gets hired at Yanna Technologies. His goal isn't to micromanage; it's to ensure every employee understands the organizational culture and its vision, having heard it straight from the founder and CEO's mouth.

As Louay Eldada of Quanergy Systems, Inc., began to build his executive team, he did so slowly and without promising prestigious titles. As an experienced founder, Eldada has learned to avoid hiring people simply because they have the talent and titles. He says, "If someone doesn't buy into the vision and want to be part of it regardless of title, I don't want them here."

5. GET OUT OF THE WAY SO OTHERS CAN SUCCEED
According to Nido Qubein of Highpoint University, an effective leader is a person who creates capacity in others. One of the most important ways to accomplish this is to get out of the way and allow others to own the work that they do.

Each Sunday night, Sheila Jordan reviews her calendar to decide what things she can shed rather than try to control. She looks for tasks and meetings that her team members can take care of, with an eye to getting out of the way and bringing up someone else who is ready for the next challenge. This not only helps her to develop leaders but to make the maximum impact with her own time.

6. BUILD A SOLID NETWORK OF RELATIONSHIPS
The leaders we interviewed for this book all understood that success depends upon a network of relationships. In fact, Hala Fadel of Leap Ventures advises emerging leaders not to do anything until they build a network of support. Most leaders described networks that include individuals within their organization and individuals external to it. Such networks provide knowledge, problem-solving advice, emotional support, mentorship, and more.

The story of Raj Puri's career progression highlights how building and maintaining relationships is an essential leadership behavior. Puri built a business plan at Booz Allen Hamilton in cooperation with people from Illuminet. Years later, Puri launched a product at VeriSign—with the original core of people, only to continue the journey at Yanna years later.

7. BUILD STRATEGIC PARTNERSHIPS
Boards of directors, customers, suppliers, and venture capitalists are all stakeholders who can be strategic partners contributing to an organization's success. Especially

in times of crisis, these partnerships, if handled well, can make all the difference in the world.

Rosina Racioppi of WOMEN Unlimited, Inc. says, "In good economic times and bad, we build deep strategic relationships with our partners. We understand that when they are successful, we are successful."

During the economic downturn, WOMEN Unlimited made adjustments, such as delaying invoicing and creating low cost ways for customers to continue working with them. This allowed partners to stay involved with the organization without losing ground until the budgets bounced back. As a result, the organization did not lose even one of its corporate partners.

8. CARE FOR AND REWARD YOUR PEOPLE

Every leader we interviewed proactively seeks to communicate care and concern for the people who work for him or her. When Rana el Kaliouby of Affectiva needed to energize her team for a major change in direction, she was successful, in part, because of the relationships she had already built. She had demonstrated interest in her team members' personal lives and families. el Kaliouby's team members knew that while she cared about Affectiva, she also cared about them. She was known to sometimes take off her *Affectiva hat* and put on her *Rana hat*, endorsing a change that was good for an employee and a loss of valuable talent for Affectiva.

Sheila Jordan of Symantec believes that people are the single most important asset in any company. She says:

> *I have to manage budgets; but I'll never, ever, ever underspend on merits or bonuses. I'll spend every dollar I can and go fight for it, and I think I have a reputation for that. But, yes, I have a high expectation or bar for myself, and I expect the same of people that I work with.*

9. OVER COMMUNICATE WITH ALL STAKEHOLDERS, ESPECIALLY IN TIMES OF CRISIS OR CHANGE

Consistent communication is essential in every business climate, but in times of crisis, change, and uncertainty, it becomes even more important. Our participants spoke with conviction about the need for transparency, consistent messaging, and stepping up to tough conversations.

When David Martin was hired at Cardiovascular Systems, Inc. (CSI), his job was to take the fledging private company public. No one expected the economic downturn that came in 2008, when the company was ready to make the move. Suddenly, Martin's job became helping the company survive the downturn. Martin committed himself to communicating with every audience: directors, executive team, employees, investors, physician partners, etc. Each audience involved challenging conversations.

For example, some of CSI's top engineers said:

> *Hey, I've got kids and I'm uncertain about what's going to happen here. I have an opportunity to work with a big company. If I go over there, I know they will never tell me I can't get a paycheck. I can't say that if I stay here.*

Martin was honest about the reality that a missed payroll could happen at CSI. He told the employees that he was committed to the mission of improving the lives of those at end-stage vascular disease and described the steps the company was taking. Martin believed that those who stayed did so, in part, because of the candor. With knowledge, they could embrace the challenge and accept the risk. These folks became loyal employees and part of the story of CSI's success.

Communicating vision and business realities is one aspect of leadership communication. Communicating performance feedback is another. Our participants were deliberate in setting standards and providing feedback about performance.

10. BUILD TRUST AND BUY-IN

Prith Banerjee of Schneider Electric joined the company with a mandate for change from the CEO. He knew he could quickly develop an idea or insight about what was happening in the company and formulate a plan. That plan, however, would be perceived as Banerjee's plan, not belonging to the people who were needed to implement it. Knowing that trust and buy-in are essential elements for successful change, Banerjee traveled around the world, visiting sites and conducting town hall meetings. He says:

> *Believe me, if town hall meetings are about building trust, then they are about listening, listening, listening—because the best ideas for the organization are actually sitting inside the people who work for the company. They know what the problems are. They do this work every year. So, I will extract the things I need to know from these town hall meetings.*
>
> *I went to Shanghai and to Bangalore to listen. I traveled like crazy for about three or four months. Then I worked with the CTOs to create a strategic plan. I orchestrated the plan, but it was the leaders' plan. The CTOs think, "This is our plan."*

WHY IS THIS IMPORTANT FOR YOU?

Communication is a skill and art you can learn, and it qualifies as one you need to succeed as a leader. And, as with any skill, you must exercise communication to become good or great at it. If you're willing to work at it, you can rapidly improve the quality of every part of your life. The fundamental steps include starting with a plan, communicating with frequency, and delivering a consistent message over time.

Communication is critical for building alignment and executing strategy. Yet it is often one of the most challenging leadership skills because it is so easy to talk about, but not so easy to do. Effective communication is far more than a one-way street that starts with the leader.

When it's working, communication is the leader's "information highway," flowing freely in both directions and in every circumstance—in good times and, especially, in challenging ones.

As you read the pages of this book, you'll see that effective leaders believe that sharing information is critical, but it is substantially less than half the battle. Yes, you must communicate clearly about the organization's strategy, speed, direction, and results. But you cannot stop there. Verbally and nonverbally, the way in which you communicate—humbly, passionately, and confidently—has more impact than the words you choose.

The leaders represented in this book inspire others through their words and actions. And before they speak, they listen and observe. To them, knowing the audience is as important as the message they want to deliver.

In the pages that follow, you'll see how leaders use communication to inform, persuade, guide, and assure, as well as inspire. You'll see how they've learned to reveal more of themselves and let others see their souls.

WHY IT IS IMPORTANT
FOR YOU TO READ THIS BOOK

The leadership communication stories you'll read in this book will help prepare you to communicate during times of crisis as well as how to rally others to embrace opportunities. As you read the different leadership communication cases, you will see that regardless of the company size or industry, all leaders grapple with the issues of getting everyone (employees, investors, board members, etc.) on the same page. This is one of the hardest ongoing tasks for any leader. How great is it to have an insider's view on how 12 successful leaders have done just that!

Our goal is to help you navigate the waters with strategies, tactics, and tools that the leaders we interviewed will provide you throughout this book. The real-world case studies, told in interviews by the leaders themselves, will provide a better education than any theoretical textbook. As you move from chapter to chapter, you'll find a summary of each chapter, with lessons learned and space for you to write and reflect on the insights you had during your reading.

If you are a current or aspiring leader hungry to learn how effective leaders have managed and led organizational change and initiatives through word and action, you'll find a treasure trove in this book. If you want to learn from their example, review tested communication strategies, and see what steps you can adopt and emulate in your own environment, you'll find this book a practical resource. If you want to think about human relationships and organizational dynamics—at employee, leadership team, and board levels—as well as chart a path to communicate to create alignment when stakes are high, you'll have an exciting journey in these pages.

Let's get started!

SHEILA JORDAN
Senior Vice President and Chief Information Officer,
Symantec Corporation

As Symantec's CIO, Sheila Jordan is responsible for driving the company's information technology strategy and operations, with a focus on building and supporting the global information technology effort. She led the transition from outsourcing IT at Symantec to building an internal organization to serve the company's IT needs. During the process, Symantec decided to separate its businesses, creating an even greater challenge in the face of a hard deadline.

Prior to joining Symantec, Jordan spent nine years at Cisco, where she served as SVP of IT, Communication and Collaboration. She was responsible for delivering and integrating key IT services for Cisco's global workforce, including the development of the company's WebEx Social Collaboration platform, as well as the deployment of all emerging technologies. Jordon also led mobility services and desktop strategy, in addition to launching Cisco's internal app store for mobile that provides transactional applications.

A frequent speaker about collaboration, mobility, Bring Your Own Device (BYOD) issues, and women's leadership, Jordan also has held leadership roles at The Walt Disney Company and Martin Marietta.

She received her Bachelor of Arts degree in Accounting from the University of Central Florida and her Master of Business Administration degree from the Florida Institute of Technology.

CHAPTER 2

SHEILA JORDAN

When Steve Bennett, then CEO of Symantec, hired Sheila Jordan to become the company's Chief Information Officer (CIO), he gave her a task of removing an obstacle. Several years earlier, the board of directors had decided to outsource the company's IT function.

For a number of reasons, including changes in leadership, the strategy wasn't working. In fact, Bennett described IT at Symantec as an impediment to the business. When Jordan talked to Bennett about her concept of IT in three categories, he explained that even the most basic component was riddled with problems.

In Jordan's view, you can think, somewhat simplistically, of a company investing in technology to run the business, change the business, or grow the business. Bennett said, "I can't get to change or grow because there are so many issues with running the business." Obviously, Jordan would need to make things change—and fast.

Jordan came to Symantec from Cisco, where she had spent eight years as Senior Vice President (SVP), IT, Communication and Collaboration. Given that Jordan views herself as a change agent who understands how technology can add value to a business, the role at Symantec was a good fit for her. She brought her passion and ability to inspire and motivate a team to collaborate across the organization.

Successful Change Begins with Assessment

Jordan entered Symantec planning to measure change in quarters because she knew she could demonstrate progress and show how change can happen in 90-day increments. During the first quarter, she assessed the situation and the existing team. Jordan says:

> *The most important thing to do as a leader walking into an organization is to create the best leadership team you can possibly find. That will just cascade throughout the organization. When you're new to a company, the decisions you make about people are watched, and it sets the tone of the organization, and I mean all decisions. Whether it's who you hire, who you decide to terminate, or who you decide to promote. Those decisions, when you first walk into an organization, are carefully watched.*

Jordan wanted to elevate and promote some existing people, and she knew she had to make decisions on exiting some others. She also wanted to bring in some talent with a fresh perspective.

A top priority was to ensure that the IT organization belonged to the team rather than to Jordan or the CIO. To this end, Jordan walked the team through an exercise she has used with other teams. She began by convening the team with the task of structuring the organization. She presented an organizational structure, with no names in the boxes. Then Jordan asked, "Do you agree? What are we missing? What are we not missing?"

People who had been with Symantec a long time responded with their own ideas and insights. Together, the team created the organizational structure together. The task took about seven revisions and two and a half weeks. Everyone involved owned the structure.

Once the structure was set, Jordan asked the existing staff to tell her which jobs they wanted, prioritized as 1, 2, or 3. Some staff members felt comfortable answering within the group; others preferred to give their answers in private. Both ways were respected, and Jordan learned a great deal in the process. Even in situations in which a fit was obvious, she learned the team member's interests and ideas of growth. This provided opportunities for development.

Only two jobs were in conflict, and these were solved quickly with a discussion. The result was a leadership team in place quickly, within 35 days. Most important, the team members owned the organization.

LEADING A CHANGE
INVOLVES PERSUADING THE PLAYERS

Fortunately, for Jordan and her team, there was no internal resistance to the decision to insource IT. Of course, an inherent conflict existed between the new IT team and the companies that had been providing IT services under the old model. Jordan admits to having been nervous about that. She knew she was extracting a significant amount of income from each outsourcer, and yet she needed them to help her complete the job at hand.

The first couple of months were daunting, and the outsourcing companies were uncertain about how serious Symantec was about the project. Finally, Jordan had conversations that went something like this:

> *Listen, we are going to do this. This is why we were hired. This is real. Here is the plan. You really have one choice: Do you want to help me with insourcing or not? You'll end up getting some additional work, keeping, or maintaining some.*

> *I'm not going to take everything in. There are some things that make sense to have someone else do, and you*

*can choose to be that person or not. It's going to depend
on how you choose to help me insource.*

Fortunately, the companies understood the logic, and they
proceeded with what Jordan calls an "amicable divorce." The
outsourcing companies stepped up and are today a considerable partner in Symantec's ecosystem.

SUCCESSFUL CHANGE
REQUIRES CONTINUAL COMMUNICATING

To meet the urgency of getting an insourced IT up and running, Jordan found herself quickly hiring a new team of employees with the technical competencies that had been missing. She was working to establish a leadership team as well as
carry the tone and the culture of the new IT organization.

Like all successful leaders, Jordan appreciates the importance of communication—and of repeating important messages consistently over time. She decided to start writing a
weekly blog. Each Friday morning, she wrote a couple of paragraphs on things that were actively happening. Jordan believed this could be a way in which the IT staff could get a
sense of who she was and what she thought was important.
The blog would also help people to see how their part fit into
the bigger whole.

Toward the end of each blog, which she continues to
write each week, Jordan adds something personal. During the
football season, it's often about the 49ers, her kids playing
sports, or something else.

The comments people write back are mostly about the
sporting events. One team member asked Jordan why she only
writes about American sports. Why not talk about cricket? She
replied, "Okay, teach me about cricket, and I'll get into the
cricket team and I'll write about cricket stuff."

The blog has become a powerful communication vehicle for the IT organization. In fact, team members share it with colleagues who work in other departments inside Symantec. The blog gives them a sense of what's going on in the company.

Jordan intended to write this blog weekly throughout the insourcing. Then, when another huge wave of change hit the company with the decision to separate Symantec into two independent companies—one focused on storage business and one cyber security—she decided to continue the blog. Two-plus years after beginning the blog, Jordan says she has missed only two weeks of writing when she didn't think she had a useful update to share. On both occasions, she received urgent messages from readers asking when she planned to publish next.

SUCCESSFUL CHANGE AGENTS
ENSURE BUSINESS RESULTS

When Jordan came to Symantec, the company was spending a considerable amount on IT, more than the benchmark averages. Some of the money, of course, went to the outsourcing vendors. Additional money was spent by other parts of the company who sought alternative solutions because they weren't getting quality service from Symantec IT that met basic standards.

Saving money was a motivating factor in choosing to insource, but Jordan also had to deliver more reliable service. As you'd expect, the company has many indicators to measure IT service, including frequency and duration of outages.

With the entire company as their customer, Jordan and her team seek to optimize services across the organization every quarter. Sometimes that means cost reduction. Other times it means spending a little more to deliver better quality.

LEADERS DRIVE
CHANGE AND GROWTH IN OTHERS

From Jordan's perspective, leadership is about followership at every level. Leadership is not a title, but the way a person shows up and drives change. She says, "You can't be a leader unless you are positioning something or you're structuring something that people want to follow."

According to Jordan, people don't work for companies, they work for people—and they expect a lot from their leaders. People want to follow someone who is inspiring, aspirational, and motivational. They want to feel valued and confident that their leader genuinely cares about them. People want to work for leaders who challenge them and stretch them to become better. They also want to know that the person they work for will support them. They want to be confident that if they make a mistake, the leader will have their back and help them to develop and grow. Jordan says:

> *People are the most important thing. I'll run through fire, walls, and everything else for people. Companies sometimes forget how important people are, and I think the single most important asset in your company, regardless of what vertical or business you are in, is the people. At the end of the day, everything, every expense item you see, every revenue number you see, has people behind it. They are the ones that make things happen at the end of the day.*

While Jordan cares about people, she's a tough boss. Team members describe her as the hardest boss they have ever worked for, but by far the one who has most helped them develop in their careers. She says:

> *I think my team members feel that they're cared for. I know I have a reputation that I take care of my team. I have to manage budgets; but I'll never, ever, ever underspend on merits or bonuses. I'll spend every dollar I*

can and go fight for it, and I think I have a reputation on that. But, yes, I have a high expectation or bar for myself, and I expect the same of people that I work with. My husband would describe me as completely impatient, and I schedule to the left. If there's a schedule and a date, I want it done earlier and more urgently. My team would probably say that, too.

When Symantec decided to separate its companies, Jordan and her team were faced with a hard deadline. They were still building the IT infrastructure when they were charged with preparing for separation. The team had one year to get the job of separation completed.

In such a case, effective leadership calls for good decision making and the tenacity to stick with a core decision once it is made. Jordan's big question was, "How do I de-risk the plan?" She decided it made the most sense for the separated company, Veritas, to temporarily remain a customer of Symantec's IT service, just as other internal departments were customers. This allowed the IT team to concentrate on building the infrastructure without needing to separate it at the same time. This arrangement would serve all the IT customers until Veritas decided they were ready to fully separate. The board of directors and other stakeholders all agreed this could be done.

During the yearlong process of separating, consultants and others challenged the decision, but Jordan remained confident in her strategy despite all the second-guessing. To serve her customers and meet the looming separation deadline, Jordan needed to set the direction and keep her team focused. Jordan says, "In moments of leadership like that, you've just got to summon the courage to stay the course, and overly communicate."

With her plan for separation in place, Jordan motivated her team by breaking the project up into 90-day increments. She branded each period with a memorable tag line to create a sense of urgency and inject some fun into the process. There was March to March, Drive to December, and Jump to June.

Time was so limited that Jordan daily drilled into her team a favorite mantra: "Seconds matter." Any delay threatened to create a major domino effect that could cost the team a week or more of productivity. The mantra gave people permission to be more assertive than usual and take action. It became natural for people to walk over to a teammate or pick up the phone and ask how they could help remove an obstacle. The awareness that every second matters ensured the project stayed on track.

LEADERS BUILD A NETWORK
FOR KNOWLEDGE AND SUPPORT

When asked who she turns to for advice, leadership, and mentoring, Jordan replies, "Everyone and everyone." While she may say this tongue-in-cheek, she also means it. Jordan claims to have an amazing network, and she advises every professional to build such a network as early as possible in his or her career.

For starters, Jordan has an e-mail list of roughly 30 Chief Information Officers (CIO) in the Silicon Valley. The group is collegial, and they share stories and ideas with each other on a regular basis. Jordan knows five or six so well that she will pick up the phone when stuck and ask what the others think. These people in her network share her challenges.

Jordan also has a network of women leaders whom she talks with regularly about matters unrelated to technology. She urges women to make a commitment to networking—not to let it slide because of the "second job" at home. The investment in relationships with your peers is critical. Jordan says:

> *We think it's great to go to that networking event. Then the day of, something happens and we have to take care of the children...or something unexpected happens, and*

we think it's more important than the networking we had planned.

Men don't cancel. Men golf. Men do it. Men think golf-ing and networking is a part of their job. I suggest to women, "Don't cancel." Do whatever you can, but put a networking event on your calendar on a quarterly basis or monthly basis, and don't cancel it. One reason is that, yes, you want to network. You want to become known and all that. The second reason for me, now, is that I love to pay it forward. I love to go and just help others. I'm a connector, so I love to connect people. All the people that helped me, I want to pay it back, and I just think it's really important to do.

In addition to CIOs and a network of women leaders, Jordan builds lasting relationships with providers and other influential stakeholders. Once the insourcing was complete within Symantec, she wrote letters to the top 20 vendors who helped her through the process. She wrote to the CEOs and their teams to thank them for what they had done for her team in the effort. Now all these connections add to the network that continues to be a resource and support to Jordan.

ADVICE TO EMERGING LEADERS

Jordan has definite ideas about how to grow as an emerging leader. Here are some of her top suggestions:

1. DO YOUR JOB WELL, AND THEN RAISE YOUR HAND
   Doing your job with excellence is foundational, and that should be every professional's top priority. Until you have that right, you are not ready for extra activities. Once you have built a foundation of excellence, Jordan suggests you sign up for anything and everything!

   Every organization has some type of major task force going on. By participating, even in a small role, an emerging leader begins to understand and align with the priorities of the company. Such experiences also help an emerging leader to build a network within the organization.

2. UNDERSTAND THAT LEADERSHIP IS NOT A TITLE—LEADERSHIP IS INFLUENCE AS AN INDIVIDUAL

You can find many opportunities in areas outside of work that connect with your passions. These are great places to build skills. It might be a church group or social activity, and it might be an organization with bad leadership. There's a lot to learn, even if it's knowing exactly what you don't want to be.

3. WORK HARD AND PLAY HARD

Jordan believes she is a successful mother as well as a successful leader because she balances work and play. It's important to figure out when it's time to go and play hard and put work aside. Jordan believes this is not only important, it is critically important.

4. PRIORITIZE YOUR TIME

The only thing that doesn't change in life is the 24 hours everyone gets each day. To become an effective leader, decide what is important, and spend your time and energy on those items. For Jordan, it's all about impact. She says, people ask me how I prioritize. I have an impact filter, and I think, "If there are 10 IT people going to that meeting, I don't need to be there. Where do I need to spend my time that I'm going to have the most impact for the company versus being in a face-time meeting to gain exposure and whatever else people go to meetings for?"

Every Sunday night, I look at my calendar and decide what things I need to shed rather than try to control. What things can I shed that I can have my trusted team do, and/or bring up someone else who is ready for the next challenge? I'm constantly thinking about what I can do with my time to make an impact.

* * * * *

It used to be that technology was the run-the-business, stand-behind-the-curtain type of role in organizations. This is no longer true. As an example, Jordan shares a conversation she had with the CEO of an airline industry. The CEO said, "I'm not an airline company, I'm a technology company with wings." Every aspect of an airline company, from booking reservations, to tagging luggage, to landing planes relies on some element of technology.

Smart technical leaders think of themselves as business leaders who deserve and earn an equal seat at the table. Every emerging leader, regardless of function within the organization, needs to think the same way. Through functional expertise, developing people, and execution, leaders drive change that is essential to organizational success. Whatever your role, make sure it's about impact, not activity.

Summary

1. From Jordan's perspective, leadership is about follower-ship at every level. Leadership is not a title, but the way a person shows up and drives change. She says, "You can't be a leader unless you are positioning something or you're structuring something that people want to follow."

2. An effective leader ensures that the organization belongs to the team rather than the leader. Jordan facilitated the process of her IT team developing its own organizational structure.

3. When implementing change, it's useful to measure performance in quarters. Demonstrate change and progress in 90-day increments. Jordan's first 90-day increment involved assessment.

4. Successful leaders appreciate the importance of communication—and of repeating important messages consistently over time. Jordan accomplished this, in part, with a weekly blog.

5. People don't work for companies; they work for people. It's a leader's job to make sure his or her people feel cared for and supported. Among other things, people want to be confident that if they make a mistake, the leader will have their back and help them to develop and grow.

6. In times of challenge, a leader needs to summon the courage to set the direction, stay the course, and over communicate.

7. Leaders develop networks and stay active in them. They don't let other responsibilities crowd out this aspect of their job. Jordan's network includes stakeholders as well as peers who share her IT challenges.

8. In the face of many demands, a leader must prioritize time. Each Sunday night, Jordan looks at her calendar and considers which tasks she can shed.

9. As a path to growth, Jordan recommends building a foundation of excellence in your job and then raising your hand for extra activities.

YOUR NOTES AND REFLECTIONS

_____

_____

_____

_____

_____

_____

_____

_____

_____

_____

_____

_____

_____

_____

Dr. Nido R. Qubein

Seventh President of High Point University,
Entrepreneur, Award-Winning Speaker,
and Philanthropist

Dr. Nido R. Qubein became the seventh president of High Point University (HPU) in January 2005. By all measurements, he has led HPU through an extraordinary transformation, including the following, listed on the HUP website:

- Significant and measurable academic growth
- 210% increase in traditional undergraduate enrollment
- 178% increase in faculty
- 367% increase in campus acreage
- And dozens of additional strategic growth accomplishments

Qubein came to the United States as a teenager with limited knowledge of English and only $50 in his pocket. His inspiring life story is one filled with adversity and abundance. He earned his Bachelor's Degree in Human Relations from High Point University in 1970, and his Master of Science Degree in Business Education from the University of North Carolina at Greensboro Bryan School of Business & Economics in 1973; in 2009, he was awarded an Honorary Doctor of Letters in Humanity degree from the University of North Carolina at Greensboro.

Qubein has authored dozens of books and audio programs distributed worldwide. He is the recipient of multiple awards.

CHAPTER 3

DR. NIDO QUBEIN

When Nido Qubein returned to his alma mater, High Point University, as the seventh president, he brought 30 years of entrepreneurial, corporate, and business leadership experience with him. A charismatic personality, Qubein had founded and run successful businesses; won the highest honors in professional speaking; and founded a philanthropic foundation, among other accomplishments. But was he up to the task of leading an academic institution? Would his business perspective help him lead the university into a prosperous future—or squash its soul?

When Qubein assumed the role of president in 2005, he knew he had to act quickly. He had a pivotal opportunity and a pivotal challenge. As a small and unknown private university, High Point had to stand on its own. Without the ability to attract students, the school had no revenue and no way to pay its bills. To make matters worse, the country was in the middle of its worst recession in 50 years.

By 2015, a mere decade later, it was clear that, with Qubein at the helm, the university had achieved spectacular success. Here are some statistics, cited on the university's website that prove the point:

	2005	2015	Growth
Undergraduate Enrollment (Traditional Students)	1,450	4,400	203%
Fulltime Faculty	108	277	156%
Campus Size (acres)	92	410	346%
Square Footage	0.74M	4M	441%
Buildings on Campus (new and acquired)	22	112	409%
Total Positions	430	1,433	233%
Economic Impact	$160M	$464M	190%
Operating and Capital Budget	$38M	$290M	663%
United Way Giving	$38,000	$225,000	492%
Study Abroad Programs	5	56	1,020%

Obviously, Qubein did not accomplish all this on his own. Qubein says the following:

> *What lies behind these impressive statistics is a university fully dedicated to continually enhance its academic programs and ensure that every student receives an extraordinary education in an inspiring environment with caring people... We owe respect and appreciation to our family of faculty and staff who deliver on this promise every day.*

While faculty and staff deliver on the High Point's promise to students every day, Qubein leads the charge. His ability to inspire such performance stems from his definition of leadership and his personal frame of reference.

Qubein defines a leader with one short line: A leader creates capacity. He explains:

> *An effective leader is a person who creates capacity in others, capacity to do more, to learn more, to be more, to give more. The truly transformative leader, versus a transactional leader, is the one who understands relational capital.*

> *At the end of the day, there are five kinds of capital: financial capital, reputational capital, educational capital, physical capital, and relational capital. I argue that besides physical capital, your capacity to walk here, see, and have good health to do what you need to do, besides that, relational capital is the most important.*

As we all do, Qubein approaches leadership from a frame of reference based on his life experiences. One of the earliest pivotal points in his life occurred when his father died when Qubein was only 6 years old. His mother, who had no formal education, but a great discipline of common sense, had to reinvent herself in order to feed and clothe her five children. Observing his mother as he grew up, Qubein learned principles for life and living, as well as fundamentals that later helped him in business and relationships. One of the most salient of these is that there is no end to the road, that there are always possibilities.

Another pivotal experience that has shaped Qubein's frame of reference happened after he arrived in America as a teenager. Born in the Middle East, Qubein came to America with $50 in his pocket, looking for a better life. Qubein attended a small, two-year school and struggled to pay his way. As he was ready to graduate and move on to a four-year school, Qubein learned that he owed the school more money than he had realized. He was worried.

An anonymous doctor from a neighboring city donated the difference on Qubein's behalf. This experience provided a pivotal moment from the perspective of stewardship and philanthropy. According to Qubein, a leader is a steward that creates capacity in people. The doctor unknowingly created within Qubein the capacity to do more, to be more. This experience affected more than his knowledge of leadership; it affected his soul. Qubein says:

> *I went back to my dorm, knelt by the side of my bed, cried my eyes out, and that day made a commitment to God that someday, I too, would somehow help someone to go to college. This was the impetus for the Qubein Foundation, where we've helped some 700 students in the last 30 years to go to college. This came out of that one incident where I made a commitment. You make a decision with your brain; you make your commitments with your heart. That's why commitments are longer lasting; that's why they are harder to break.*

LEADING THE TRANSITION AT HIGH POINT

Qubein's leadership is best defined by his clear and deliberate focus. When Qubein took the job at High Point, he understood that four essential things would need to take place to ensure transformation. The university needed:

1. A clear vision
2. A solid strategy
3. Practical systems
4. Consistent execution

Without a clear vision, it's difficult to lead people toward a better future. Qubein knew he needed a simple statement, one that people could easily comprehend, and one that Qubein himself could repeat often. Here is the vision statement that has propelled the university forward: At High Point University, every student receives an *extraordinary education* in an *in-*

spiring environment with *caring people.* Qubein embraced this statement because he could repeatedly drive home this message with conviction.

Every time he speaks, Qubein talks about extraordinary education and the components that comprise such an education. An extraordinary education has the following components: holistic education, experiential learning, and values-based living. He talks to people about what it means to provide an inspiring environment—and what it means to be caring in relationship to students.

To embody the vision fully, the organization had to be re-cultured. In other words, new patterns of thinking had to be introduced and take root. Everyone needed to focus his or her energies on the vision. The effort manifested itself in a variety of ways.

As an example, consider the vision that everyone on campus will interact with students as caring people. A good beginning is for faculty to act in caring ways, but that's not enough. To change the culture, Qubein changed the messaging typically used for other roles on campuses.

On most campuses, people who work with food are known as food service workers. Qubein changed the message, saying, "You don't work in food service; you lead hospitality." When a student comes to any of the 14 restaurants on campus, the workers are expected to host that student as if the restaurant is a home. It's a completely different mindset.

In similar fashion, landscapers, plumbers, electricians, painters, and maintenance people are now in the role of campus enhancement.

Once the vision is clear, an organization needs solid strategy. This is the second component in transformation. In other words, the organization must answer the following questions: Where am I today? Where do I want to be? How do I get there?

Third, an organization needs practical systems. Qubein believes that effective leaders understand that measurable results come to those who are practical and pragmatic. This doesn't mean the leaders aren't innovative, but that they avoid leading their people down paths that are excessively risky or might be unachievable.

Finally, to achieve its best, an organization needs consistent execution. If it's worth doing, it must be done repeatedly. Qubein says, "If the speech I gave about extraordinary education, inspiring environment, and caring people is important to our existence and survival, then I must do it again, and again and again and again. It never gets old. It's what we stand upon, what we live for, and what we believe in."

At High Point, several application points support the vision, strategy, systems, and execution. For starters, average is out; a commitment to excellence is in. In Qubein's view, excellence is defined as relevance—and the recipient, not the distributor, always defines relevance.

In addition to striving for relevance, the university now competes with its differences, rather than its traditional strengths—because strengths are simply the prerequisites to being in the game at all. High Point University strives to position itself in ways that stand out from other universities.

The final application point involves moving from a fixed mindset to a growth one. A growth mindset doesn't rely on what's been done in the past or what others do. It explores, expands, and inspires the organization to become radically better all the time and in whatever arena. To plant seeds of this mindset in people's hearts, Qubein came to High Point saying, "We are not in the business of training. We are in the business of education. Education means to change from within. That meant that we don't really want teachers; we want enablers of learning."

Faculty and staff members at High Point are encouraged to plant seeds of greatness in the hearts, minds, and souls of the students. They strive to model values that are worthy and worthwhile for students to emulate. With this perspective, amazing things happen. The desired transformation in the lives of students doesn't come with a lecture; it comes through a modality of living.

INTRODUCING CHANGE TO
AN ESTABLISHED ORGANIZATION

Established in 1924, High Point University had a long history before Nido Qubein stepped in as president. Given that Qubein was an entrepreneur and businessperson, it's natural that some people would be frightened. In addition to change itself, they might fear that a businessperson, however success-ful, wouldn't understand scholarly practices or achievements. Faculty might fear being viewed as employees rather than learned individuals. They might fear arbitrary budget and staff cuts for the sake of short-term numbers.

Introducing change is a pivot point for the leader and the organization. Qubein's approach was to talk about the fear, acknowledge it, and address it directly. Of course, talking isn't enough; he also modeled it. In time, people saw that Qubein wasn't behaving in the ways they feared. In fact, he was talk-ing about how they could create a team that made something happen at the university. He encouraged teamwork and mod-eled a can-do attitude and a belief in the art of the possible.

In saying things like, "There are no such things as unreal-istic dreams, there are only unrealistic timelines," Qubein works to create capacity in others, his very definition of lead-ership. He encourages people to look deeper within them-selves to discover the very best of themselves and to do the very best they can do.

Of course, this approach won't work for everyone, and Qubein is pragmatic about that. If 80 percent of the universi-ty's employees catch the energy of possibility, extraordinary things can happen. The other 20 percent won't get moved up or get the biggest assignments. They still belong, are still respected, and still perform worthwhile jobs. They just don't move up.

When Qubein took up the mantle of President, he looked at the broad picture of the university as a puzzle. His first step was to take an inventory of who was there and what they were capable of achieving. He was interested in a person's capability and asked himself questions regarding each: What is this person's capacity to make something happen? Is this someone I can count on?

He identified half a dozen young people who were capable, committed, willing to learn, and willing to be coached. Today, each of those individuals is a senior vice president at High Point.

An example of his coaching, Qubein taught these individuals about decision-making. He taught them to consider the primary and secondary elements of each decision. For example, when deciding how to operate the campus transportation system, the primary element is the best interest of the student. The secondary elements are things like logistics, cost, etc. Putting the student first in every single decision influences the soul of the university and has propelled it forward.

Once Qubein had assessed internal capabilities in the university, he asked himself what pieces of the puzzle were missing. In places where he didn't have the internal capacity needed, he went outside, either to outsource or employ. Internal and external pieces had to be arranged to make the correct puzzle. In other words, people had to be moved into the right positions to achieve something Qubein calls intentional congruence.

Intentional congruence is based on goals, aspirations, and a future view. These elements ensure the organization gets the results it's looking for at the end of the day. And, of course, the elements must constantly be reassessed, examined, improved, and realigned. Ultimately, the job of leadership is to think, not to do. The leader thinks, and then eventually brings a team around to practically and pragmatically accomplish what is needed.

COMMUNICATING STRATEGIES, PRINCIPLES, AND MINDSETS FOR SUCCESS

The messaging about roles of food service workers and landscapers is one of many strategies, principles, and mindsets that Qubein introduced to re-culture High Point. Here are some of the others:

1. FOCUS ON PREPARING FOR THE WORLD AS IT'S GOING TO BE, NOT THE WORLD AS IT IS, NOR THE WORLD AS IT WAS

   Obviously, no one can precisely predict how the world is going to be, but it is possible to surmise, with some accuracy, a number of the qualities a person will need to survive, and thrive. High Point focuses on preparing students to compete and collaborate in an ever-changing, fast-moving marketplace that is no longer continental, but rather global, in nature.

2. UNDERSTAND THE DIFFERENCE BETWEEN VALUE AND VALUE INTERPRETATION

   Qubein believes that many leaders misspeak when they talk about the need to create value. While people want value, "value alone does not own the key that will unlock the door to greater opportunities." If you want to open such doors, you need to have expanded capacity, ability, and knowledge—and be proficient in value interpretation.

   You must interpret value from the perspective of the receiver in ways that the receiver finds meaningful and purposeful in his or her life. If you fail to interpret the value from the receiver's point of view, you end up talking from your own perspective, which doesn't have power to interest or engage your receiver.

3. **DEVELOP YOURSELF AS A
FOLLOWER AS WELL AS A LEADER**
Leadership and followership are partners. If you hope to be an effective leader, you must also be a lifetime learner, a lifetime student. This means that you are being coached as well as coaching. You are following your own heroes, models, and mentors.

When asked about his own mentors, Qubein explains that he appreciates and learns from different people for different reasons, business and personal. For example, he follows the philosophy of Scottish theologian William Barclay when it comes to giving. Barclay says we should always give without remembering and receive without forgetting. To Qubein, this is about more than money; it's about all your resources, talents, and abilities. "Always give without remembering" is a huge mantra in Qubein's life.

Qubein also follows Mother Teresa. She is a mentor in terms of sacrifice and humility, balanced with an amazing ability to administer, produce, execute, and make things happen. Mother Teresa ran a big organization.

4. **DEVELOP FAITHFUL COURAGE**
Qubein believes that transformational leaders have a combination of faith and courage. The faith isn't only religious faith; it involves belief in what you are doing, the path you are taking. When you combine faith and courage, you have a terrific combination.

Leaders who have faithful courage have confidence, but not the type based on motivation, although motivation is important. The most effective leaders have confidence based on competence. Qubein looks for leaders whose competences are so congruent with the nature and purpose of the organization that they lose themselves in faithful courage. What's more, they develop this capacity for faithful courage in others.

5. DEVELOP AN ENTREPRENEURIAL SPIRIT
    People with an entrepreneurial spirit are flexible, nimble, courageous, and aware. They may or may not be an entrepreneur; in fact, a minister, teacher, or person in any job may possess an entrepreneurial spirit.

    The goal for graduates from High Point University is to embody an entrepreneurial spirit by being a job creator rather than a job taker. A job creator isn't necessarily a person who opens a business and hires new people. A job creator may be a person who is so effective in performing a job as an employee that he or she creates greater opportunities for the organization. Such performance directly or indirectly begins to create more opportunities for others.

6. STRIVE TO DEVELOP VERTICAL
    AS WELL AS HORIZONTAL THINKING
    Horizontal thinkers are people who take matters at face value. We might view them as problem solvers who think in terms of time management. Vertical thinkers, on the other hand, are people who look deeper and are more incisive in their thinking. We might view them as solution finders who think in terms of energy management. There's a measurable difference between the two.

    This distinction is particularly important in a university setting, because horizontal thinkers believe that training is the measure of learning. Vertical thinkers understand that education is the measure of learning. To illustrate, a trainer will teach a child to count; an educator will teach a child what counts.

Here's another way to look at the distinction: Horizontal thinkers are people who have *to do* lists. Vertical thinkers are people who have *to be* lists. Vertical thinkers strive to become the people they need to be to in order to achieve the things they desire. Qubein explains:

> *So many people live by their to do list: I must do this. I must do that. I'm not saying anything negative about this. We all have to do lists. Every day I have things I must get done. I must go to this meeting, call this person, write this letter, and read that report.*
>
> *These tasks alone do not get me to the fullest meaning of life. The fullest meaning of life comes from the vertical thinker who asks, "To accomplish these things naturally, with minimal energy, and create the best results, what kind of person should I become?" Then the doing flows naturally to me. The question is, what is on my own to be list?*

In order to formulate a *to be* list, a person must first formulate a *stop doing* list. To become, or grow, you have to change, to transform. This is only possible if you stop doing something and create room for something new.

Qubein gives an example involving weight loss. Imagine you want to lose weight and know that your daily habit of eating chocolate bars creates a weight problem for you. It doesn't make sense to formulate a goal saying, "I want to become healthy and manage my weight," and leave it at that. You must formulate a *stop doing* goal that says, "I will quit eating three chocolate bars a day." Something good might come of that.

Things on the *stop doing* list for effective leaders include stopping the focus on leading processes and managing time as top priorities. Effective leaders need to focus their energy on creating capacity, inspiring, and growing people. They must begin to develop systems and environments in which people are inspired to get the job done. In this way, leaders multiply themselves many times over. This is what Qubein means by capacity: individual capacity and corporate capacity. Leaders create cumulative capacity.

To make things even more challenging, Qubein introduces another element:

> *Ultimately, the best leaders are not horizontal thinkers or even vertical thinkers. The best leaders are diagonal thinkers. By diagonal thinkers, I mean they have the ability to see and observe things horizontally, and they have the capacity and the ability to analyze and dissect things incisively in a vertical way, but then they have this magical skill to merge the two and begin to feed into the other. They arrive at conclusions and see things that come naturally to them. Those same things seem magical to an outsider who cannot comprehend how it's so easy for the leader to see or do this.*

Qubein is an exceptional communicator; a person who can articulate the principles and strategies behind his success on a 30-year career. This includes his decade at the helm of High Point University, previous business successes, philanthropic leadership, and his career as the highest caliber professional speaker. So many inspiring and insightful points stand out. Among the ones we might remember when we face our own pivotal points of crisis or opportunity include believing in possibility, being a lifelong learner, fostering a belief in what you are doing, and living by your *to be* list rather than your to do list.

ADVICE TO EMERGING LEADERS

At High Point University, each freshman takes a course called Life Skills, taught by Qubein. In the past, companies treated college graduates as apprentices, and carefully groomed them for a lifetime of service and loyalty. As this is not true in our economy, High Point provides this course early in a student's career. A testimony to the importance of these skills is evident in the fact that Qubein teaches the course himself.

The elements of the course, provided on the High Point website, provide advice for all emerging leaders. (We've adjusted each description to provide the action step "learn how to..." rather than a course objective).

1. LEARN HOW TO GAIN A POSITIVE SELF-ESTEEM
   Positive self-esteem can give you the character to face any obstacle that stands in your way. With high self-esteem, you can meet the most disappointing and discouraging situations with faith, hope, and courage. The primary difference between winners and losers is attitude. Winners make their goals; losers make excuses.

2. LEARN THE ART AND SCIENCE OF GOAL-SETTING
   Most of the things that make life worth living require careful introspection, sufficient time to develop, and plenty of hard work. Setting goals and consistently working toward them is the only way to control your life.

3. LEARN THE FUNDAMENTALS OF LEADERSHIP
   Leaders are made, not born. Even if you don't want to pursue a career that is traditionally thought of as requiring leadership, you can certainly benefit from

knowing how to persuade, influence, and negotiate with others.

4. LEARN THE IMPORTANCE OF FISCAL LITERACY AND STEWARDSHIP
Make the effort to learn how to manage your own money for long-term prosperity. Know how to save, invest, avoid bad debt, and otherwise make sound financial decisions.

5. LEARN THE IMPORTANCE OF HEALTH AND WELLNESS
What is more central to quality of life than quality of health? There's no point in having a brilliant, purposeful career if you don't feel well enough (or live long enough) to enjoy it.

6. LEARN THE BASICS OF TIME MANAGEMENT
Time is your greatest treasure. If you don't make a constant decision to invest it in the pursuit of your goals and objectives, you are throwing your time away. Learn practical techniques for analyzing your time habits, keeping daily and weekly *to do* lists, getting organized, and yes, making time for leisure, friendship, and spiritual growth.

7. DEVELOP EFFECTIVE COMMUNICATION SKILLS AND DELIVER PERSUASIVE PRESENTATIONS
Through effective communication, we exchange information, ideas, and opinions with other people; we integrate our lives into the human race, and we make happen the things we want to happen. Communicating effectively is the "master key" to success.

SUMMARY

1. Qubein defines an effective leader as a person who creates the capacity in others to do more, learn more, be more, and give more. Thus, a leader multiplies himself or herself, leading to widespread transformation.

2. Four essential things were needed at High Point to ensure transformation. The university needed 1) a clear vision; 2) a solid strategy; 3) practical systems; and 4) consistent execution.

3. When crafting a vision, Qubein searched for a simple statement, one that people can easily comprehend, and one that he could repeat with conviction often. To embody the vision, the leadership team re-cultures the organization to match it.

4. The ultimate job of a leader is to think, not to do. The leader thinks, and then eventually brings a team around to practically and pragmatically accomplish what is needed.

5. To develop your own leadership capacity, consider the following:

   - Prepare for the world as it's going to be, not the world as it is, nor the world as it was.

   - Understand the difference between value and value interpretation. Interpret value from the perspective of the receiver in ways that the receiver finds meaningful and purposeful in his or her life.

   - Develop yourself as a follower as well as a leader. If you hope to be an effective leader, you must also be a lifetime leaner, a lifetime student. This means that you are being coached as well as coaching.

   - Develop faithful courage. This involves belief in what you are doing, the path you are taking. When you combine faith and courage, you have a terrific combination.

- Develop an entrepreneurial spirit. People with an entrepreneurial spirit are flexible, nimble, courageous, and aware, whether they are entrepreneurs or not.

- Strive to develop vertical as well as horizontal thinking. Horizontal thinkers are people who take matters at face value. Vertical thinkers, on the other hand, are people who look deeper and are more incisive in their thinking. There's a measurable difference between the two.

- Stop asking yourself what is on your *to do* list and ask yourself, "What's on my *to be* list." In order to formulate a *to be* list, you must first formulate a *stop doing* list. To become, or grow, you have to change, to transform. This is only possible if you stop doing something and create room for something new.

YOUR NOTES AND REFLECTIONS

_____

_____

_____

_____

_____

_____

_____

_____

_____

_____

_____

_____

_____

_____

_____

_____

_____

_____

_____

_____

_____

_____

_____

_____

DR. PRITH BANERJEE
Executive Vice President, Chief Technology Officer, and
Member of the Executive Committee,
Schneider Electric

Dr. Prith Banerjee is the EVP, CTO, and member of the Executive Committee of Schneider Electric, reporting to the Chairman and CEO. In this role, Banerjee is responsible for driving innovation and technology differentiation as well as coordinating the R&D activities of the company across its five businesses, including 11,000 R&D personnel, and a €1.3 billion R&D investment.

Banerjee has previously served as the Managing Director of Global Technology of R&D at Accenture, CTO and Executive Vice President of ABB, SVP of Research at HP, and Director of HP Labs. He has also served as the Dean of the College of Engineering at the University of Illinois at Chicago.

He is a fellow of the AAAS, ACM, and IEEE and a recipient of the 1996 ASEE Terman Award and the 1987 NSF Presidential Young Investigator Award.

Banerjee holds a Bachelor of Technology Degree (President's Gold Medalist) in Electronics Engineering from the Indian Institute of Technology, Kharagpur, and a Master and Doctorate Degree in Electrical Engineering from the University of Illinois, Urbana.

CHAPTER 4

DR. PRITH BANERJEE

It's never easy for an outsider to come into an organization and initiate significant change. The outsider typically faces mistrust and resistance every step of the way. When Prith Banerjee joined Schneider Electric with a mandate for change from the CEO, he was the very definition of an outsider. He was from a different culture, ethnicity, and industry. Fortunately, Banerjee had been an outsider before, and he had learned from some mistakes. He was prepared to embrace the challenge.

Schneider Electric is the global leader in sustainable energy management and industrial automation. Headquartered in Paris, the French company is a €27 billion company, with five businesses and 150,000 employees in 100 countries. The first business provides low-voltage products for residential buildings, commercial buildings, and large critical infrastructure buildings. The second business involves medium-voltage dealings with utilities, small grids, and more. The third business works to automate processes in oil and gas, metal, wastewater, and more. The fourth business is a data center business. The fifth is a large research and development group, employing well over 10,000 people.

Each of these businesses has its own Chief Technology Officer (CTO) who runs IT direction for that business with a dotted line back to Banerjee.

Schneider Electric, which has been in business for 180 years, has a massive global footprint. The company was doing well when Banerjee came on board, but it wasn't growing as quickly as the CEO wanted it to grow. The CEO hired Banerjee from outside to spearhead change.

At the time of this writing, Banerjee has been with the company slightly less than one year. The long-term results of his efforts are not yet in, but there is still a lot we can learn from his story. Banerjee was brought in as a member of the executive team, reporting to the CEO. With one exception, all the other leaders are French. Banerjee is from the United States, of Indian origin, from the Silicon Valley. He looked different, he spoke a different language, and his experience was in different industries. Why would others believe Banerjee had the solution for innovation and growth? He says, "If I were a French employee sitting inside Schneider Electric, I would immediately throw Prith out the window." He describes his challenge as follows:

> Just think about the challenge that I am facing. So here is the CEO, he'll say, "Prith, go figure things out and come back with a precise plan." He basically says, "My employees don't know how to grow the company. You are in Silicon Valley; you are supposed to know. You worked in various IT companies. I have not hired you to be an expert in the industrial space. I'm hiring you from IT space. Tell us what to do."

> How was I to gain the trust of the people in this company? If I just aligned with the people, I have not done my job for the CEO. If I aligned just with the CEO, it would be like saying, "You guys don't know anything, and I am the guru of this advisory board."

> This is the challenge: An outsider coming into a leadership role with a company that sees itself as fantastic, doing wonderfully. Actually, it was a great company, a great brand, but it was kind of stuck on growth. It was not growing.

Before coming to Schneider Electric, Banerjee was Managing Director of Global Technology R&D at Accenture. Earlier, he was Chief Technology Officer and Executive Vice President of ABB Group. Before that, he was Senior Vice President of Research at Hewlett Packard and Director of HP Labs.

Prior to entering the corporate world, Banerjee spent 20-plus years in academia. He made the shift because of frustration he experienced as a professor of electrical and computer engineering at Northwestern. Banerjee and his students were developing great technologies, but they weren't having success transferring the technologies from academia to the consumer. This problem led Banerjee to found AccelChip, Inc., a developer of products and services for electronic design automation.

He served at AccelChip as president and CEO, raising $2.3 million in financing, helping the company build its first product, and guiding the company's growth to 25 employees and $800,000 in revenues before moving on.

LEADERS INVEST IN LISTENING TO AND LEARNING FROM THE PEOPLE WHO DO THE WORK

With his variety of experience, Banerjee knew he could quickly develop an idea or insight about what was happening in Schneider Electric. He could conduct a quick assessment and come up with a plan. That plan, however, would be perceived as Banerjee's plan, not belonging to the people who were needed to implement the plan. Such a scenario is a recipe for mistrust and resistance.

Trust and buy-in are essential elements for successful change. So, Banerjee traveled around the world, visiting sites and conducting town hall meetings. He thrived in the big R&D groups that had 800 or 900 people, including all the R&D engineers, attending the meeting.

Banerjee opened those meetings by saying, "I have no PowerPoint. I'm here to listen and to learn." The communications office protested, claiming that Banerjee didn't know the company culture. He was too new and might get wrong ideas in the process.

Banerjee had achieved good results in town hall meetings he had conducted in the past, and he persisted in his method. He explains his process this way:

> *Believe me, if town hall meetings are about building trust, then they are about listening, listening, listening— because the best ideas for the organization are actually sitting inside the people who work for the company. They know what the problems are. They do this work every year. So, I will extract the things I need to know from these town hall meetings.*
>
> *I went to Shanghai and to Bangalore to listen. I traveled like crazy for about three or four months. Then I worked with the CTOs to create a strategic plan. I orchestrated the plan, but it was the leaders' plan. The CTOs think, "This is our plan."*
>
> *Each of the businesses had a plan that belonged to them. At every meeting, I said, "It is your plan. I am just an outsider. I'm the orchestrator." At every meeting, I said multiple times, "I am an outsider. I know nothing about it. You guys can do it. All I will do is be the judge."*

In addition to the town halls, Banerjee met one-on-one with the CTOs of each of the five businesses that make up Schneider. He made a special effort to learn from and create alliances with these leaders. Banerjee readily acknowledged that he was new to the company and business. He expressed his desire to learn from those who had experience there.

For example, he reports the following conversation with a CTO named Clemens:

> *Clemens, remember I wanted to have this mentoring session, in which you are my mentor. I would like to hear from you, "Am I doing the right things or not?"*

For two hours, we had a very open dialogue about, "Hey, I'm doing this. Am I on the right track? You have been at Schneider for 30 years. What advice would you give?"

I say, "Look, I don't know anything," which is true. I really don't know that business. In response, people immediately want to help because they believe I'm willing to listen and learn.

LEADERS CREATE BUY-IN WITH QUESTIONS AND SUGGESTIONS, NOT WITH DECREES

The skill in driving successful change, of course, isn't what you know; it's your ability to guide leaders to recognize their problems and generate the solutions themselves. By asking pointed questions, Banerjee was able to guide leaders to develop and take ownership of their own strategic plan.

For example, Banerjee learned that the company had a not-invented-around-here syndrome. Some employees confided, "We're at Schneider. We're very smart and we try to build everything ourselves."

In response, Banerjee mentioned that some well-known companies participate in open innovation, which rests on the belief that advancing an organization's technology is best accomplished by using external as well as internal ideas and paths to market.

Had the team heard of open innovation? Did they think it should be in the plan? Banerjee provided options in the form of questions rather than advice or demand. After some discussion, in which the team asked Banerjee what he thought, they decided open innovation should be in the strategic plan. Introducing the concept as he did allowed Banerjee to ask a question when he knew the answer.

In another example, Banerjee reviewed a number of portfolio projects and discovered that the bulk of the projects were short-term. He told the team, "Look, if you do only short-term, how do you think you can get out of this mess? Obviously, we are stuck in this low growth because you are not investing in the future."

Rather than decree a solution, Banerjee asked the group what they thought they should do in the face of this information. They looked at a number of short, medium, and long-term distribution of projects in other companies and decided on a distribution of their own. The idea to do more long-term than short-term R&D appeared to come from the group, but Banerjee had served as a guide and facilitator to get them there—where he knew they needed to go.

When it was time for Banerjee to present the strategic plan to the executive committee, he was able to say, "This is not my plan. It is the plan of these people." Banerjee was careful to give credit to the specific people who had contributed to the strategic plan.

The executive members said, "Oh, he's my CTO! He wrote the plan." Naturally, the executives bought into the plan, and the commitment to that plan went to the top of Schneider. Those who contributed to the plan looked like winners and reaped the benefits from that perception.

Banerjee's first six months at Schneider Electric focused on winning trust and getting people on board with the strategic plan. Then it was time for execution. At the time of this writing, Banerjee has been at Schneider less than a year, and it is too early to show definitive results. Still, Banerjee is excited about the journey and the progress that is evident already.

The technology group has already transformed into an open innovation organization. They are working with a number of startups and seeing the value of open innovation. This represents an early success, one that allows people to see progress based on the strategic plan.

LEADERS LEARN AND GROW FROM THEIR MISTAKES

Because this book is intended for leaders, Banerjee was eager to share the lessons he learned from big mistakes. The first lesson: Avoid imposing your solutions on others, even when you are confident you are right. Instead, learn to ask the right questions.

Before he began working in industry, Banerjee was what he calls a "hardcore academic," a professor. He had been Department Head of Electrical Engineering at Northwestern, and the Dean of Engineering at University of Chicago. He describes one of his early experiences in the corporate world:

I came in, I said, "This is it." You see, the trouble with being a professor is you are a professor. You are teaching to students and the students love listening to the professor because the professor is supposed to know and students accept that they have a lot to learn. My mistake was not realizing that people in corporations don't have the same perception as students. I came in from the academic world not being an arrogant person, but I was used to lecturing and people listening to me. I came into a corporate environment and faced a lot of resistance. I'm confident I had the right ideas, but people said to each other, "Prith, the professor, is coming in and telling us X, Y, Z. What does he know? He's only from academia." I had to do a lot of damage control in that situation.

I learned the most important way to build any relationship is to get trust. Even if you think you know the answer, don't say you know the answer. You have to extract that answer out of the people from the organization and make it appear it is their plan. Trust and buy-in are such important things.

I attribute some of the positive reception I've already received at Schneider to listening. For example, when I did a town hall in Bangalore, people were posting on

social media sites for Schneider Electric, "Oh wow! We
found this energetic guy. He's listening to us. He's not
like the other executives. He's actually not afraid of
tough questions."

Another mistake Banerjee made was to go against his commitment to authentic communication. In one of his corporate
leadership positions, the company had decided to make cuts
across the board. In his roles in academia, Banerjee had handled such situations with town hall meetings, where he explained that if he had to make a cut, how he was going to go
about it.

In the corporate setting, this approach met the resistance
of internal strategists. They said, "You have to cut, but word
cannot go out that we are cutting because then the stock market will punish us."

Rather than speaking honestly at a town hall meeting,
Banerjee found himself speaking stiffly from a script that im-
plied people were being let go because they were poor per-
formers. He made a statement and did not take questions. He
tells the story this way:

Typically, when I do town halls, I go out there and am
always open, joke with people, and interact with them.
Now I give this talk and bolt out of the room. I had just
announced that a hundred people would lose their jobs
because they are lousy people.

I got a lot of hate mail that evening, and I thought,
"What the hell did I do?"

After some introspection, I realized I had taken bad ad-
vice. I talked to my boss and then did a week's worth of
damage control. I came out very openly about what had
happened and was able to win back trust. Boy was that a
lesson learned.

ADVICE TO EMERGING LEADERS

When asked for advice for emerging leaders, Banerjee recommends making a conscious effort to learn and to connect:

1. PAY ATTENTION TO WHAT
   OTHER COMPANIES ARE DOING
   Banerjee believes emerging leaders in many companies are too internally focused. Because their businesses are running on treadmills, these leaders don't take time to attend external meetings to learn what other companies are doing. Yet, leaders grow best when they are learning from external as well as internal sources.

   At Schneider Electric, Banerjee may suggest a book, model, or event featuring an outside leader to his technology group. Examples include Geoffrey Moore's book *Zone to Win* and John Kimball's spinning model. The purpose is to explore the questions: What are other companies doing? What might we consider doing differently? What ideas can challenge us to think differently?

2. REACH OUT TO LEADERS IN YOUR
   ORGANIZATION AND ASK FOR ONE-ON-ONE TIME
   People tend to be afraid to reach out to senior executives, especially in big organizations. Banerjee reminds us that senior executives are just human beings. You can expect a senior executive to be busy, but most will also find the time to talk with you—if you ask. If you are only reaching out to junior people, you are not doing enough.

3. EXPAND YOUR NETWORK
   At company events, deliberately sit with people who are not your peers. Build a variety of connections. Introduce yourself to others—and to the CEO. Reach out to senior people and let them know you. You don't have to come up with a way to impress

the senior people; just get to know them in an authentic way.

4. BE AN ANSWER PERSON
    RATHER THAN A COMPLAINER
    If you introduce a problem, suggest a solution. Leaders hear problems all the time, and they aren't impressed. If you suggest a solution and ask for an executive's reaction, that executive will notice you. Ask questions and engage in authentic dialogue.

Banerjee is a man with a big job at a big corporation. He is poised for success because of his skills, insights, and experience—and perhaps most important, because he has been willing to learn from past mistakes. One of Banerjee's biggest lessons is that successful leaders cannot successfully force change. Leadership is about building trust, extracting knowledge from team members, and facilitating plans for change that team members can own.

SUMMARY

1. When introducing change, a leader can expect resistance, especially if that leader is brought in from the outside. That resistance can be expected to grow if the leader imposes his or her solutions on the organization.

2. An experienced leader might be able to make a quick assessment of a business situation and make a plan to move forward. Such a plan, however, would be perceived as the leader's plan, not belonging to the people needed to implement the plan. Such a scenario is a recipe for mistrust and resistance.

3. Trust and buy-in are essential for successful change. At Schneider Electric, Prith used town hall meetings as his method to listen, learn, and build trust. He was careful in those meetings to acknowledge the expertise and knowledge of those who worked in and understood the business.

4. Leaders create buy in with questions and suggestions, not with decrees. By asking pointed questions, Banerjee was able to guide leaders to develop and take ownership of their own strategic plan. Banerjee presented himself as the orchestrator rather than the composer of the plan.

5. Banerjee made a special effort to learn from and create alliances with the CTOs of each of the five businesses that make up Schneider. Banerjee readily acknowledged that he was new to the company and business. He expressed his desire to learn from those who had experience there.

6. When it was time for Banerjee to present the strategic plan to the executive committee, he was able to say, "This is not my plan. It is the plan of these people." Banerjee was careful to give credit to the specific people who had contributed to the strategic plan.

7. Leaders grow best when they are learning from both internal and external sources. Leaders need to attend external meetings and pay attention to what other companies are doing.

8. Young professionals need to reach out to senior leaders in the organization and ask for one-on-one time. Those who are reaching out only to junior leaders are not doing enough to build their networks.

9. Banerjee recommends becoming known as an answer person rather than a complainer. Leaders hear problems all the time, and they aren't impressed. When someone suggests a solution and asks for an executive's reaction, the executive notices and remembers that person.

YOUR NOTES AND REFLECTIONS

_____

_____

_____

_____

_____

_____

_____

_____

_____

Hala Fadel
Managing Partner at Leap Ventures
and
Founder and Chair of the
Enterprise Forum of the Pan-Arab Region

Hala Fadel co-founded Leap Ventures in 2014 and has been a managing partner with the firm since then. She has 20 years of experience in finance and entrepreneurship. She was a portfolio manager for 12 years in European Equities at Comgest, a €20 billion growth equity fund focused on investing in growth companies. Prior to that, Fadel started Booleo, a telecom software business, later acquired as an internal solution by a client.

Fadel started her career in 1996 at Merrill Lynch in London, working in mergers and acquisitions. She is the founder and chair of the MIT Enterprise Forum of the Pan Arab Region, an organization that promotes entrepreneurship and organizes, among other things, the MIT Arab startup competition.

Fadel graduated from HEC in France in 1997 with a Master in Financial Economics and attended the Berkeley Haas School of Business. She holds a Master of Business Administration from the MIT Sloan School of Management.

CHAPTER 5

HALA FADEL

For Hala Fadel, the life-changing shift in her career came in the form of a question from her husband, "Are you happy?"

Her husband was ready to support Fadel, if she was happy in her secure job at Merrill Lynch London, but he noted that Fadel, age 27 at the time, didn't seem happy. From his perspective, Fadel seemed tired, and she was becoming boring.

Realizing that she had become boring was a personal crisis for Fadel. With so much of her life still ahead of her, Fadel wasn't willing to accept such a reality. In a 2011 TEDx Beirut talk, Fadel explains her response to this question that shook her world. She quit her job and enrolled in MIT to earn an MBA. The year was 1999, during the height of the Internet bubble. It seemed everyone was starting a company, and the viral energy surrounding startups "caught" Fadel. She came up with an idea to decrease the costs of telecommunications in banks and presented her idea to the MIT 100K Business Plan Competition.

Thanks to the competition, Fadel's company gathered a team that got funded, got clients, and grew to 10 employees. Fadel's story was even featured on the front page of the *Boston Globe*. A client later acquired the company as an internal solution. Fadel, meanwhile, had become hooked on entrepreneurship.

Life took another turn when Fadel moved with her husband to Lebanon. Although she was Lebanese, Fadel had grown up in Paris and had little exposure to Lebanon. She explains her experience in moving to Lebanon:

> *I was totally depressed by the environment. I saw there
> was no energy, no sense of initiative. People did not take
> the initiative to start something or to change things,
> even things they didn't like. It seemed they thought these
> things weren't worth fighting for.*

LEADERSHIP INVOLVES ENERGY AND MINDSET

Fadel wanted to avoid this kind of mentality, in herself and in her children. She remembered the energy that had surrounded her in Boston, thanks to what she calls "the entrepreneurship ecosystem" and the MIT startup competition. At MIT, Fadel had caught a vision for entrepreneurialism and was mentored and pushed to pursue that vision. The energy and the process was anything but boring. She wanted that again in Lebanon, for herself and others.

Fadel believed that Arab youth deserved an environment with the same viral energy and support that had been so important to her. She decided against complaining and in favor of doing something about it—and she started the MIT Arab Startup Competition. Fadel's vision: To ensure that every Arab who had a good business idea and passion would get the help he or she needed to start the company.

In 2005, Fadel teamed up with a few other entrepreneurs from the region to begin the competition. She was advised not to expect much interest, given that nobody in the region would understand what the competition was all about. The group started the competition with $15,000 in sponsorship money, plus the $50,000 cash prize. They expected between 100 and 200 applications.

That first year, the competition received 1,500 applications. Despite appearances, young Arabs were hungry to be entrepreneurs, but no one was helping them get started.

Getting that first competition under way was challenging, because everything was scaled for 200 applications. Fadel began reaching out to more judges to review the applications. Her dedication was such that many of the calls originated from the hospital, where she had just delivered a child. Friends from school, the Arab network, and the MIT network responded. They were all amazed to discover so many entrepreneurs from the region and were ready to help. Although the Middle East and North Africa (MENA) region reportedly doesn't support women, Fadel found a few men who genuinely supported the initiative and her. Fadel salutes these individuals and counts herself lucky to have found them, especially as an Arab woman.

Once the competition got through that first challenging year, they focused on figuring out how to scale the effort to reach out to more entrepreneurs. Originally, the goal was more on changing the mentality in the region rather than on actually creating businesses. A few years down the road, when they had critical mass, the goal shifted.

MARKETING AN ENTREPRENEURIAL MENTALITY

The move toward entrepreneurship begins with the belief that you can have power over your own life and can even change a region. In the course of marketing this mentality, Fadel was put in touch with the people who think differently within the Arab region. She learned that while the "dark side" gets all the attention and airtime, the "bright side" is there too. People were ready to create change; they simply needed empowerment.

With this realization, Fadel experienced her biggest life turning point yet. She decided to quit her job of investing in growth companies in Europe after 20 years. She decided to pursue this work in the Arab region by co-founding Leap Ventures with a team of serial entrepreneurs.

Leap Ventures is a venture capital firm that looks to make investments in innovation and technology startups from the

MENA region. The organization works with companies that have established a market presence and are looking to accelerate their global market penetration and commercialization.

The formation of Leap Ventures allowed Fadel to mesh her volunteer work with the MIT Enterprise Forum (a nonprofit) with her day job (a for-profit startup). Up until this point, her extensive work with the competition had been gratis. By the sheer force of her belief in the competition and powerful leadership communication, Fadel was able to take it to the next level. She certainly wasn't boring anymore!

A team of eight now runs the MIT Arab Startup Competition, which is itself a successful startup. From its beginning in 2005 with a small sponsorship, the competition has experienced impressive growth. Today, the competition receives 5,000 applications from 20 Arab countries. The competition features three tracks: ideas, startup, and social entrepreneurship. Most important to Fadel is the change in mentality this growth represents. While mentality is difficult to quantify, it's important to Fadel, because it's the essential component to make entrepreneurship succeed.

LEADERSHIP TRAITS FOR SUCCESS

Fadel's story points to exceptional leadership, including the ability to communicate in ways that attract others and turn her passion into organizations that energize and benefit others. While Fadel is reluctant to prescribe a leadership style or appear pretentious, we can glean the following recommendations from her story and her comments.

1. BE INCLUSIVE OF EVERYONE
    Fadel has a background and perspective that allows her to be uncommonly inclusive within the Arab region. Where it's common in the region to think of yourself as Lebanese, Egyptian, or Saudi, Fadel embraces the identity of the whole.

Having grown up outside of the Arab region, Fadel was accustomed to being perceived as Arab, rather than from a specific country in the region. Her mother is half-Egyptian; Fadel is Lebanese; her father worked in Saudi Arabia when Fadel was a young girl; and her aunt lives in Palestine. When she returned to Lebanon, Fadel thought of herself as Arab. She says:

I was equally interested in Alexandria, as I was interested in Dubai, as I was interested in Kuwait, as I was interested in Syria. I was able to connect with people from different countries and include them in this project. This is what made the project work. I reached out and people believed I was interested in their own ecosystem. This pulled it all together and made people want to help.

To be able to put together a panel, event, or institution, you need to be inclusive of everyone.

Fadel's inclusivity naturally extends to women as well as men. She is naturally a champion for women, and she feels lucky to have found men in the region who support Arab women. The MIT Enterprise Forum employs eight women and works with many more. Fadel notes that women in the Arab region are perceived as apolitical. This perception makes it easier for women than for men to knock on doors on behalf of a nonprofit.

2. COMMUNICATE YOUR MINDSET, ENERGY, AND VALUES

The initial spark that ignited Fadel's work with The MIT Enterprise was all about mindset—creating environments of energy and support for change and entrepreneurship. Only after communicating and establishing the mentality could the competition begin to focus on creating profitable companies. Today the mentality of the MIT Startup Competition has become a mixture of both.

With Leap Ventures, of course, Fadel is investing in companies for profit, so she puts her energy into creating success stories in the region. Much of the work still involves mentality. Fadel explains:

Entrepreneurship comes with a certain mentality; it comes with a set of values. You value teamwork and the private sector. You seek to create a company and make it big, create employment, and share the success of the company with your employees. You are inclusive, you come to work on time, and if you don't like something, you just change it.

Promoting entrepreneurship is promoting these values. This is exactly what we need in this part of the world. Promote entrepreneurship, and as a side product, you help the region transform its values and mentalities.

3. WORK LIKE A SLAVE, RULE LIKE A KING, AND CREATE LIKE A GOD

    CEOs of successful startups don't act like CEOs. They act like people who will do any job, from using the copier, to cleaning floors, to working with clients. Successful entrepreneurs shed their egos and get to work. Fadel claims this is good news, "because you don't need ego for anything."

    Hard work is essential, but a business won't succeed without leadership skills. No one can build a successful business alone. "Engaging and motivating people to work requires as much leadership skill as a king during wartime."

    Everything in today's world is open to intense competition. Whatever idea you have; you can be sure someone else is working on it too. Fadel's advice:

"Shoot for the moon and create like a god from day one." That's the route to success and the personal satisfaction that comes with being your own boss.

Fadel's TEDx talk is titled "God Is an Entrepreneur" because of an insight from Fadel's daughter. Hearing Fadel rehearse this speech, her daughter remarked, "God must have been an entrepreneur because he created us and everything else."

4. **BUILD A VILLAGE AROUND YOU**
Referencing Hillary Clinton's idea that it takes a village to raise a child, Fadel encourages entrepreneurs to build a village or network of support around themselves. She explains:

> *The formula is to create a network around you that will be a network of love, affection, energy, money—people who will support you no matter what. I feel so privileged to be surrounded by such people. If you don't have this, it's easy to create it, especially in this part of the world. People are willing to bond with you on a cause. . . I would say don't do anything before you have this support because it's a tough journey.*

5. **FOCUS ON ONE THING**
The world is full of projects and opportunities, each with someone promoting it to you. While it's easy to chase after various opportunities, the path to success requires singular focus. Being known for one thing allows your village to support you. Otherwise, you have to build multiple villages.

This doesn't mean you are limited to one enterprise. Fadel runs the MIT Leadership Enterprise, is Managing Partner at Leap Ventures, and has an initiative working to empower youth and their projects. The cause behind each, nonprofits and for-profit, is empowering others to be entrepreneurs.

6. Give back
    Fadel identifies empathy as a critical leadership
    trait. Part of her success in the Arab region is her
    sincere empathy for countries, situations, and indi-
    viduals. Empathy drives you to act in support of
    others. Fadel believes it's important to give back
    early in life, and she certainly has demonstrated this
    in action. Her original work with the MIT Enter-
    prise Forum was as a volunteer. Only later did she
    figure out how to intersect the Forum with her for-
    profit work in Leap Ventures.

    The MIT Startup Competition has recently added a
    social entrepreneurship track, a trend that is emerg-
    ing across the world. The fact that it's new every-
    where gives the Arab region an advantage. And the
    fact that the Arab world has so many problems pro-
    vides opportunity for social entrepreneurs in that
    part of the world. The drive for action in solving so-
    cial problems mirrors Fadel's original commitment:
    "When you see a problem, find a solution."

Advice to Emerging Leaders

Fadel's advice to emerging leaders is clear from the passages
above. When asked what she tells her son and two daughters
about growth and good citizenship, Fadel answered, "I don't
tell them, I just bring them along with me. I take them to the
MIT Enterprise Forum events so they can see it for themselves. I think telling, especially today, is the worst way to
teach something. They have to see it and experience it for
themselves."

Other pieces of advice include the following:

1. Don't do anything until
    you've built a network of support
    Accomplishing things as an entrepreneur is tough,
    especially if you are a woman. On down days, it's

good to be one phone call away from warm words of support.

2. BUILD EMPATHY AND INCLUSIVITY
When individuals, groups, and regions believe you are concerned for their well-being, they respond in positive ways. Sincerity will win the day.

3. STRIVE FOR FOCUS AND
IGNORE THE NOISE AROUND YOU
Knowing there will always be more projects and demands, Fadel keeps herself focused by reminding herself, "I can only be good at one thing." Focus and humility allow you to have consistency, which allows you to nurture a network that knows and supports you.

4. MAKE HARD WORK A HABIT
It's foolish to expect things to be easy. It's foolish to allow your ego to limit what you are willing to do. The more you know, the less ego you should have.

Fadel's passion is entrepreneurship and the energy that surrounds it. When she didn't find an environment conducive for entrepreneurship in the Arab region, she created it, using leadership communication, inclusivity, and hard work. Fadel is convinced that each of us can identify our own passion and make incredible things happen. In fact, Fadel says to each of us, "Build a village around you to go and conquer the world."

Summary

1. The move toward entrepreneurship begins with the belief that you can have power over your own life and can even change a region. While mentality is difficult to quantify, it's the essential component to make entrepreneurship succeed.

2. To pursue her vision "To ensure that every Arab who had a good business idea and passion would get the help he or she needed to start the company," Fadel teamed up with other entrepreneurs from the MENA region to start the MIT Arab Startup Competition in 2005. Although the MENA region reportedly doesn't support women, Fadel found a few men who genuinely supported the initiative and her.

3. The initial spark that ignited Fadel's work with the MIT Enterprise was all about mindset—creating environments of energy and support for change and entrepreneurship. Only after establishing the mentality could the competition begin to focus on creating profitable companies. Today the mentality of the MIT Arab Startup Competition has become a mixture of both.

4. A key feature of Fadel's success is inclusivity. Although she is Lebanese, Fadel grew up in Paris. Where it's common in the region to think of yourself as Lebanese, Egyptian, or Saudi, Fadel always thought of herself as Arab. She embraces the identity of the whole.

5. To promote entrepreneurship is to promote certain values. Fadel says, "You value teamwork and the private sector. You seek to create a company and make it big, create employment, and share the success of the company with your employees. You are inclusive, you come to work on time, and if you don't like something, you just change it."

6. Successful entrepreneurs shed their egos and get to work. CEOs of successful startups don't act like CEOs. They act like people who will do any job, from using the copier, to

cleaning floors, to working with clients. This hard work is essential, but successful entrepreneurs also need the leadership skills to engage and motivate others.

7. Entrepreneurs need to invest in creating a network of love, affection, energy, and money that will support them no matter what. Fadel says to each of us, "Build a village around you to go and conquer the world."

8. Fadel identifies empathy as a critical leadership trait. Part of her success in the Arab region is her sincere empathy for countries, situations, and individuals. Empathy drives you to act in support of others. Fadel's original work with the MIT Enterprise Forum was as a volunteer. Only later did she figure out how to intersect the Forum with her for-profit work in Leap Ventures.

YOUR NOTES AND REFLECTIONS

_____

_____

_____

_____

_____

_____

_____

_____

_____

_____

_____

_____

_____

_____

_____

_____

_____

_____

_____

_____

_____

_____

_____

_____

_____

Dr. Rana el Kaliouby
Co-Founder and Chief Executive Officer,
Affectiva

Dr. Rana el Kaliouby is co-founder and CEO of Affectiva, the pioneer in emotion-aware technology, the next frontier of Artificial Intelligence (AI). She invented the company's award-winning emotion-recognition technology. The technology is built on an emotion AI science platform that uses the world's largest emotion data repository of nearly 4.5 million faces analyzed from 75 countries, amounting to more than 50 billion emotion data points.

Prior to founding Affectiva, as a research scientist at MIT Media Lab, el Kaliouby spearheaded the applications of emotion technology in a variety of fields, including mental health and autism research.

A popular TED speaker, el Kaliouby was recognized by *Entrepreneur* as one of the "7 Most Powerful Women to Watch In 2014." She was inducted into the "Women in Engineering" Hall of Fame, received the 2012 Technology Review's "Top 35 Innovators Under 35" Award, was listed on *Ad Age's* "40 under 40" and received *Smithsonian* magazine's 2015 American Ingenuity Award for Technology.

el Kaliouby holds a Bachelor of Science and Master of Science in Computer Science from The American University in Cairo and a Doctoral Degree in Computer Science from the University of Cambridge.

CHAPTER 6

DR. RANA EL KALIOUBY

Having left her home and family in Cairo, Egypt, to pursue a Doctorate in Computer Science at Cambridge in 2001, el Kaliouby was frustrated at the limits of technology for communicating emotions. While technology allowed her to communicate news and ideas to her family members back home, the emotions surrounding the ideas were left open to interpretation; el Kaliouby couldn't be sure that her emotional messages were being received as she intended.

Chances are el Kaliouby's sense of frustration was heightened because, at the time, she already believed that computers should be emotionally intelligent. She had already caught a vision in which computers could decode facial nuances, interpret the emotions those nuances expressed, and communicate intelligently in light of them.

While perusing graduate studies at The American University in Cairo, el Kaliouby had encountered a book titled *Affective Computing* by Rosalind W. Picard, founder and director of the Affective Computing Research Group at the MIT Media Laboratory. The MIT lab is an interdisciplinary research laboratory devoted to projects at the convergence of technology, multimedia, sciences, art, and design.

Dr. Picard is a pioneer in the field that studies the role of emotions in intelligence, communication, and relationships, as well as the possible effects of emotion recognition by robots and wearable computers.

Picard's book inspired el Kaliouby to concentrate her studies in the same field. By the time she completed a master's degree, el Kaliouby had created a prototype of a simple computer system that could read people's emotions through their facial movements.

As part of her doctoral work at Cambridge, el Kaliouby developed a computer system able to determine whether a person is interested, confused, or focused by detecting facial and head movements through a webcam or wearable camera. She became interested in possible applications in mental health, especially in how this technology could help autistic kids.

Six years after she first read *Affective Computing*, el Kaliouby met author Picard at Cambridge. In 2006, el Kaliouby joined the MIT Media Lab as a research scientist and postdoctoral researcher, and Picard became her mentor. el Kaliouby says:

I was working with the professor who started this field of research, so it was exciting for me. We were both really drawn to the social good applications of the technology. We both decided to focus on the autism applications of the technology.

Much of the funding for the Media Lab comes from industry rather than government sources. Twice a year, the Lab holds a large event for the industry sponsors, formally known as Sponsor Week. Those who work in the Lab and rely on those industry dollars for their paycheck call the event Demo-or-Die Week.

During Sponsor Week, the Lab has to demo the technology, not simply show slides. You can imagine the pressure leading up to Sponsor Week—lots of overnights, little sleep, and bursts of creative genius.

For roughly three years in a row, twice a year, the Affective Computing Research Group demonstrated the autism application technology they were working on. According to el

Kaliouby, the industry sponsors would respond, "You know, this autism work is really interesting, but have you thought about product testing, advertising, automotive, or robotics?"

Those involved in industry came to the group with many applications in mind. For example, someone from Toyota wanted to use the technology to detect drowsy driving; someone from Proctor & Gamble wanted to test the experience of shaving. The group responded by jotting the ideas on a spreadsheet and carrying on with their work in autism.

el Kaliouby remembers logging the ideas on a spreadsheet, and proceeding to do nothing about them. This is partially because, at the time, el Kaliouby had a definitive career track in mind. She was going to complete her postdoctoral degree at MIT, accept a faculty position somewhere, and spend her career in research. The path was clear in her mind, and el Kaliouby was systematically walking that path.

Then the ground shifted beneath her. At the end of 2008, Picard and el Kaliouby visited Frank Moss, Media Lab Director, in his office. They were there to lobby for 10 more research assistants for their group. The conversation went like this:

> Picard and el Kaliouby, "Frank, here is the list of 18 sponsors, and they want our technology. They are sponsors, and we can't ignore them forever because they are paying the bills. We need more research assistants in our group to service all these requests."

> Moss, "Nope. It's time to spin out."

> el Kaliouby, "What? No, I want to be faculty. I don't want to start a business. I haven't thought of myself as a business person—ever."

> Moss, "Right now, the best-case scenario for all the research you are doing is to deploy it with one school for autistic kids—or to push it at a conference. You aren't scaling this right now. If you start a company, you have

*an opportunity to make this technology change the way
we do things on a day-to-day basis."*

This conversation represented a life-altering decision point for
el Kaliouby. It was her crisis of opportunity. She and Picard
had created something with the potential to change the way
humans interact with technology. The possibilities to make the
world a better place were, and are, astounding. Would el
Kaliouby step up to the profoundly uncomfortable challenge
or slink into a conventional role and career path? el Kaliouby
says:

> *That conversation with Moss was the tipping point.
> When he talked about our technology changing the way
> we do things on a day-to-day basis, something clicked in
> my brain. I thought, "Oh. Impact. We have an oppor-
> tunity for impact."*

Together, el Kaliouby and Picard co-founded Affectiva in
2009, agreeing that the company would be a dual bottom line
business. They wanted a successful, thriving enterprise, but
they also wanted to stay true to their vision of building technology that helps people. In fact, they set up the company so
that 10 percent of el Kaliouby's personal equity, 10 percent of
Picard's personal equity, and 10 percent of the company's
capitalization table is set aside for a foundation.

After securing their first round of funding, el Kaliouby
and Picard hired David Berman, who had a background in
sales and software as a service, as CEO. Berman, too, was
drawn to the idea of a dual bottom line business—the belief
that the company could thrive and help people at the same
time. Once Berman joined the team, the company started recruiting other members and building the product. Their challenge was that the product could be applied in many different
areas, including automotive, product testing, autism, and many
more.

This led the company to cast a wide net. el Kaliouby says, "We would talk to anyone who would take our call." They got the easiest traction from advertising. The value proposition was clear to companies in advertising, and those companies were willing to buy the product.

Advertisers were struggling to measure emotions. For example, they might ask an individual in a focus group, "How does my product make you feel?"

In an effort to be polite, the individual might answer, "Awesome," when the product, in fact, made him or her feel indifferent.

In 2011, Affectiva received its second round of funding from one of the biggest advertising conglomerates, WPP. They became Affectiva's investor and their biggest client. With multimillion dollars in play, Affectiva began shifting all of its engineering and science resources to build a product for WWP. As a result, Affectiva quickly morphed into an advertising technology company, even hiring people from the advertising industry. While Affectiva was still educating and evangelizing their technology in the press, it became an advertising story.

From a science, product, revenue, and growth perspective, the results were great. Affectiva now worked with 14,000-plus brands. They had amassed an amazing database of how people express emotion, including data from 75 countries.

At some point in 2012, however, when things were going exceptionally well for Affectiva, el Kaliouby was feeling disconnected. The feeling began when el Kaliouby read a story that resulted from a media interview, and she didn't quite recognize herself. She thought, "Wow, this doesn't sound like me anymore." In the media piece, el Kaliouby heard about advertising, but not about purpose, not about her dream for the company.

At about this same time, Picard left Affectiva to start another venture, and el Kaliouby lost her business partner, personal mentor, and friend. el Kaliouby was also going through a divorce. She was sacrificing a great deal for Affectiva, working a crazy 100 hours a week. All for a company that was no longer reflecting her vision and dream.

el Kaliouby had reached another pivotal point in her life as a leader. With Affectiva's current focus, el Kaliouby had to admit to herself that the company had become an advertising technology company. Was it appropriate for her to accept this as Affectiva's reasonable evolution? If el Kaliouby didn't fit with this evolution, was it time to close the Affectiva chapter in her own life and move on?

With careful reflection, el Kaliouby realized that she believed in her original dream, not only for herself, but also for Affectiva. She says:

I actually felt that because we lost our purpose, we were hurting ourselves as a company. I felt like we were missing the big opportunity we had. Advertising was fine, but it was only one application.

... I thought we were making the wrong choice for the company, and my challenge was to show the board. I wasn't the CEO, and I had to convince our CEO.

At the time, the CEO at Affectiva was transitioning out, so el Kaliouby had to make her case to the VP of Business Development and then the new CEO. From the start, el Kaliouby had been the face of the company, the evangelist, but she had chosen not to go after the CEO position. That job now went to Nicholas Langeveld.

Sitting down with Langeveld, el Kaliouby explained that she was not doing what she came to Affectiva to do. She described some things she wanted to do, including investing in mobile technology. She communicated her conviction that the current direction of the company was hurting it.

Langeveld essentially replied, "The board is going to push back because no revenue opportunities are tied to these new verticals."

el Kaliouby was convinced the company needed to change directions, and she believed it involved investing in mobile. This was certainly a risk, because she couldn't know the outcome. She says:

> It's weird. I had this conviction that the path we were on was the wrong path. We had to find a different path. Was this new path the right one? I didn't know, but I knew for certain that the one we were on was wrong.

That fall, el Kaliouby spent most of her time negotiating and navigating. She became the gatekeeper for the company's sense of purpose.

Obviously, this was a risk both inside and outside of Affectiva—because there was no immediate revenue tied to it. el Kaliouby was able to convince the board to take the new direction, tapping into their vision of a bigger purpose for Affectiva. The board decided to take a calculated risk, but no one could predict the outcome. el Kaliouby was convinced that she was pushing for something based on logic, not just her gut. She had been watching and listening as the world was evolving in how it used technology. The need to shift to mobile was obvious, even if she couldn't immediately monetize it.

The first step of the change was to shift all of el Kaliouby's team, which was the core of the science team, and their resources. They hunkered down and got to work on mobile, which meant they didn't do all the advertising work they had been doing.

The second step was to change the company's story and perception. Langeveld was leaning in the direction of the change but he was not quite ready to sign off. el Kaliouby approached Gabi Zijderveld, the new VP of Marketing, and asked for her help. el Kaliouby closed the door, and the two created a talk track for what they wanted the world to think of Affectiva.

At the time of the change, Affectiva was known as the world leader in emotion recognition technology in advertising, a company that worked with brands and publishers.

The new positioning was that Affectiva brings emotional intelligence to the digital world. el Kaliouby and Zijderveld created a new graphic showing that media and entertainment is Affectiva's first market, but the company also does video communication and robotics. el Kaliouby says, "We built it. We almost imagined that it was happening, and we basically summarized it."

With the shift in resources and positioning, the company was implementing a new strategy, one that el Kaliouby remembers taking a good year to happen. She had to work on changing perceptions internally as well as in the media. Fortunately, the company had a good relationship with WPP, including a presence on the board. And the investment from WPP remained intact.

el Kaliouby's own team was skeptical at first. They said to her, "We've been doing advertising technology for four years. Are we really going to change?"

el Kaliouby was firm in response, "Yes. We are."

el Kaliouby's excellence in leadership shows in how she convinced her team of the messaging—and in how she energized them around the new direction. Fortunately, she had already built a foundation of trust with her team members. She had demonstrated interest in their personal lives and families. el Kaliouby's team members knew that while she cared about Affectiva, she also cared about them. She was known to sometimes take off her *Affectiva hat* and put on her *Rana hat*, endorsing a change that was good for an employee and a loss for Affectiva.

The company began to use their new messaging in all company meetings. They used the same messaging with media outlets. Soon, el Kaliouby noticed that the media started repeating the new message, even when a member of the company hadn't been interviewed. The new message was taking root.

The media perception didn't help with the skeptical team, but a good challenge did. el Kaliouby went to her team and said, "Okay, we said we are going to do mobile. Let's put a stake in the ground. Let's get all hands on deck and commit to releasing a mobile Software Development Kit (SDK) by the beginning of summer."

Of course, this challenge got a lot of push back. People and leaders said the timeline wasn't realistic; they needed more time. el Kaliouby responded, "Let's go. Let's energize everybody, motivate everybody, and let's see if we can pull it off."

The team rallied and the product was released in early August. What the team accomplished once they caught the vision was amazing. el Kaliouby says the effort has changed the whole culture of the company. People were engaged, and even the engineers who are introverted wanted to represent Affectiva. They wanted to go to hackathons and conferences and talk about Affectiva.

By the time of our writing in 2017, the strategic change el Kaliouby championed has certainly been proven correct. The risk Affectiva's board took to invest in mobile has paid off and then some.

Today, Affectiva's Affdex (emotion-aware application) SDKs enable developers to create interactive and exciting emotion-aware apps and digital experiences. Affdex SDKs capture and report emotion insights from facial expressions using any iOS, Android, or Microsoft Windows device, analyzing faces obtained from the device camera, a video, or even a single image—processed on-device and in real-time. The technology is changing how we live day-to-day as well as how we interact with computers. The applications of the technology remain far-reaching.

Affectiva is in conversation with potential partners in a range of areas. For example, they are talking with doctors in the depression space and with pain clinicians who want to be able to measure pain objectively. The company is also exploring online learning.

These markets aren't easy to navigate but the conversations are happening. Because of the visionary leadership and commitment of its co-founder, Affectiva is living out its bigger purpose. el Kaliouby isn't giving up on her dream anytime soon. In fact, she transitioned to the CEO role in May of 2016. Her passion and grit continue to make the world, as well as Affectiva, a better place.

ADVICE TO EMERGING LEADERS

1. ### FIND YOUR PASSION
    Leaders need to identify that deep-down belief that they are onto something, even when most people around them don't see it. When leaders believe their passion, they live it and inspire the people around them.

2. ### FIND YOUR GRIT
    A leader's most important quality is grit, which technically is both passion and perseverance. To succeed, you need to "pick a problem you really care about and then grind it out because it won't be easy. It is never easy."

3. ### BELIEVE IN YOUR HIGHER PURPOSE AND STICK WITH IT
    el Kaliouby changed career direction to make an impact. She then devoted herself to advocate for the bigger purpose at Affectiva, when she could have quit and moved on. She took on the role of evangelist for the company's higher purpose.

4. BUILD A FOUNDATION OF
   TRUST WITH TEAM MEMBERS
   Prior to asking her team members to embrace a new direction, el Kaliouby had demonstrated personal interest in them. She knew their interests and their families.

5. COMMUNICATE YOUR
   DIRECTION CLEARLY AND CONSISTENTLY
   el Kaliouby and the VP of Marketing at Affectiva built clear messaging about the new positioning and repeated that messaging both internally and externally.

6. ENGAGE WITH A CHALLENGE
   While el Kaliouby was the initial impetus behind the change in company direction, she engaged and energized the company with the challenge to develop a new product in record time. The resulting effort changed the whole culture of the company.

Summary

1. A person's life work can arise from frustration or knowledge of an unfulfilled need. While living in a country away from family members, el Kaliouby was frustrated at the limits of technology for communicating emotions. Fortunately, she had already encountered the work of a pioneer in the field, Rosalind W. Picard, founder and director of the Affective Computing Research Group at the MIT Media Laboratory.

2. A person's dream career isn't always the path to the greatest impact. el Kaliouby made a life-altering change in direction when she realized that starting a company would result in far greater impact than the career path she had been following.

3. Together, el Kaliouby and Picard co-founded Affectiva in 2009, agreeing that the company would be a dual bottom line business. They wanted a successful, thriving enterprise, but they also wanted to stay true to their vision of building technology that helps people. They intended to continue the work on applying their findings to help individuals with autism, their focus at MIT Lab where they worked together.

4. el Kaliouby reached another pivotal point when she recognized that the company had become an advertising technology company. el Kaliouby had to decide if it was appropriate for her to accept this as Affectiva's reasonable evolution.

5. With careful reflection, el Kaliouby realized that she believed in her original dream, not only for herself, but also for Affectiva. She felt that in losing their original purpose, Affectiva was hurting itself as a company. el Kaliouby made it her mission to convince the CEO and board to go in a new direction, which included mobile technology. At the time, the new direction represented a risk, given that it had no revenue tied to it. During that season, el Kaliouby

spent most of her time negotiating and navigating. She became the gatekeeper for the company's sense of purpose.

6. el Kaliouby and the VP of Marketing created a talk track for what they wanted the world to think of Affectiva. At the time of the change, Affectiva was known as the world leader in emotionalitics in advertising, a company that worked with brands and publishers.

7. The new positioning was that Affectiva brought emotional intelligence to the digital world. el Kaliouby carefully and consistently repeated this positioning both inside and outside of the company.

8. With the new positioning in place, el Kaliouby rallied her team around a challenge. Once the team caught the vision of quickly releasing a mobile SDK, their energy and accomplishments were nothing short of amazing. They released the product in record time.

9. el Kaliouby, whose leadership style is characterized by grit (which includes both passion and perseverance), transitioned to CEO in 2016. The board supported this move because of the importance of el Kaliouby's leadership in the science and artificial intelligence roadmap as well as in diversifying the company into other verticals outside of advertising research.

YOUR NOTES AND REFLECTIONS

_____

_____

_____

_____

_____

_____

_____

_____

_____

_____

_____

_____

_____

_____

_____

_____

_____

_____

_____

_____

_____

Dr. Ossama Hassanein

Entrepreneur, Mentor, and Venture Capitalist;
Chairman of Rising Tide Fund

Over the last 30 years, Dr. Ossama Hassanein has managed over $1 billion of international technology funds in diverse leadership roles, including those of EVP of Berkeley International in San Francisco, Chairman of Technocom Ventures in Paris, President of Newbridge Networks Holding in Canada, Senior Managing Director of Newbury Ventures, and Chairman of the Rising Tide Fund in Silicon Valley. In the eighties, Hassanein led the mezzanine financing of 80+ Silicon Valley based IT companies that became spectacular successes.

Hassanein has been chairperson or co-founder of seven leading-edge high technology startups in the US, UK, France, and Switzerland. The combined market value of these companies at exits was $2.5 billion.

Hassanein has served on the Board of Advisors of Harvard University Center for Middle Eastern Studies and UCSF Department of Ophthalmology, School of Medicine in San Francisco. He also served on the Board of Directors of Relief International, a non-profit, focusing his efforts on social entrepreneurship and women development in the Middle East. He is currently Chairperson of the Board of the Egyptian American Society and of TechWadi.

Hassanein holds a Master of Science Degree in Electrical Engineering, a Master of Business Administration in Management Sciences, and a Doctoral Degree in Electrical Engineering from The University of British Columbia.

CHAPTER 7

DR. OSSAMA HASSANEIN

W hen asked to reflect on the pivotal moments that have shaped his career, Ossama Hassanein's mind goes immediately to 1989, a year of seismic change throughout the world. A combination of crises and opportunities merged to propel Hassanein in a new direction.

The Berlin Wall fell that year, and San Francisco experienced a devastating earthquake. Apple launched the Macintosh Classic, and the idea of TED Talks took shape. The Hubble Telescope was shipped to the Kennedy Space Center, Microsoft introduced PowerPoint, and Adobe introduced its Photoshop application.

Hassanein, working in San Francisco at the time, had a connection with and strong knowledge base of a team at work at The University of California, Santa Barbara (UCSB). This particular team was one of three teams working on a project called ARPANET, which was funded by the Department of Defense.

ARPANET stands for Advanced Research Projects Agency Network. It was an early packet switching network, and the first network to implement the protocol suite TCP/IP. Both these technologies eventually became the technical foundation of the Internet.

In 1989, a pivotal moment of opportunity occurred when the Department of Defense decided to stop funding ARPANET.

Conditions after the earthquake created a personal hardship and pivot point for Hassanein. It became nearly impossible for Hassanein to get to his San Francisco office from his Los Altos home in less than two hours. This burdensome commute became an impetus to make a change. Hassanein began to think that a commute to Santa Barbara might be more manageable. Before long, he was CEO and Chairman of Advanced Computer Communication (ACC). The company, created to capitalize on the opportunity for privatizing ARPANET, consisted of 24 people with deep domain knowledge.

This pivotal moment, for Hassanein, was not only the beginning of a new voyage. He describes it this way:

This was a new understanding of how entrepreneurship, innovation, financing, corporate partnership, international expansion, customer acquisition, intellectual property, and even boards of directors—how all these things worked and how they could be better.

In 1989, California was entering a horrible recession. Unemployment was 18 percent, and the cost of real estate was dropping by 1 percent per month. At the time, Hassanein had been involved in venture capital financing for roughly seven years, with clear success in companies like LSI Logic and Oracle.

Now, as Executive Chairman of ACC, Hassanein began reaching out to people he knew who might be interested in investing in this new company. Hassanein's goal was to raise $2 million. He ended up with $40 million. Per typical practice, he appointed investors to the board of directors.

A day before the first board meeting, ACC's Vice President of Sales informed Hassanein that the company had missed the target sales number by 50 percent, down from $4 million to $2 million. It was going to be difficult to give this news to the board without arousing suspicion of misrepresentation, even though the company was growing sales at $100,000 per month.

Hassanein, whose role at the time was fundraising rather than business development, chose to deliver the tough news to the board himself. He framed the news as such, "I still don't know what has happened, but I recommend we have a follow-up meeting to discuss this. We will look backward and then look forward."

One board member responded with an obscene and threatening remark. Charlie Bass, the company's initial co-investor with Hassanein, was sitting next to him. They asked the board member to leave the room. Afterwards, Hassanein said to Bass:

This is the wrong board. Success isn't about finding faults. It's about value added. No one on this board has asked how they could help us.

As a result, Hassanein reached out to Sir Terry Matthews, a friend and founder of Newbridge Networks in Ottawa, Canada. Hassanein offered:

I have a $40 million investment. Would you like to buy out the investors at 25 percent premium and become the corporate investor? In this case, you would help the company with an OEM [Original Equipment Manufacturer] perspective.

Matthews agreed to the arrangement, and Hassanein bought out the venture capitalists that had proven to be such a bad fit. A strategic partnership was formed.

Matthews had another innovative idea. He suggested that Hassanein, in addition to being Chairman of ACC, would help Newbridge Networks to invest in companies similar to ACC. This was a completely unanticipated opportunity and another pivot point for Hassanein, one that arose from a creative, innovative response to that disastrous board meeting. Newbridge ended up investing in Juniper, Netscape, and other companies.

Reflecting on the moment when he realized that the initial board of ACC was a bad fit or worse, Hassanein describes the three possible responses that were before him: submission, confrontation, or alternatives. Submission would mean that members of the company would become slaves rather than masters of their own destiny—an unacceptable condition. Confrontation would mean focusing energy on something that might destroy the company rather than serve customers and add value. The only acceptable solution was to come up with an alternative idea.

Hassanein knew he had to dissolve the company's relationship with the initial board members, but it wouldn't be productive to kick them out. He formulated a goal to make the board members leave as winners who would be grateful—on terms that would allow Hassanein to be grateful as well. His strategy worked of buying out the original board, and, with the right board, ACC sold four years later at $285 million.

Had the original investors stayed, Hassanein says they might have learned the same lesson the new investors did. They might have learned to sit next to one another and cooperate.

Regarding cooperation, Hassanein mentions how Matt Ridley, in *The Rational Optimist,* compares sex to innovation. Ridley writes of sex as an exchange of information and cross-pollination, which enables the sustainability of biological evolution. Hassanein says:

> In the case of ideas, they meet, they mate, they mutate, and we call this learning, science, and innovation. It's always about, "What can we do together?" I had a good idea with ACC, but I needed my partner at Newbridge Networks to make that idea implementable."

SUCCESS IS FAILURE TURNED INSIDE OUT

Working together as a community is a foundational element of success. In fact, Hassanein says, "Every successful individual knows that his or her achievement depends upon a community of people working together." He believes that all of us, young and old, need a mentor to sit beside us with both head and heart. Hassanein's experience with his own parents exemplifies this sense of support and community.

In 1969, Hassanein was president of the student union at the University of Alexandria in Egypt. Furious at the military government, students engaged in a sit-in to try to understand where the country was headed. Because of his involvement in orchestrating and participating in the sit-in, Hassanein was arrested and spent four months, including his 21st birthday, in jail.

Beforehand, Hassanein knew his participation in the sit-in could be devastating to his family as well as to himself. He asked his parents how they felt about it. Hassanein's parents supported him then, as always.

When Hassanein was released from jail, he emigrated to Canada to pursue his studies, unwilling to subjugate himself to a culture of voluntary servitude in Egypt. According to Hassanein, this decisive move allowed him to be a freer man, and it also enabled him to make a bigger contribution to his country than if he had stayed under a government of oppression.

This, among other difficult experiences, qualifies Hassanein to quote from a famous poem from an unknown author:

Success is failure turned inside out,
The silver lining of the clouds of doubt
And you can never tell how close you are—
It may be near when it seems afar.
So stick to the fight when you're hardest hit,
It's when things seem worst that you mustn't quit.

In his role as a venture capitalist, Hassanein's commitment to this perspective is tested regularly. For example, through Newbridge Networks, Hassanein invested in a company started in 1996 by brothers Alex and Nicko van

Someren. The company, called nCipher, focuses on encrypting and protecting data.

At one point, Alex, who was then CEO of nCipher, came to Hassanein, distressed, reporting that the board would like to replace him. Hassanein, who was a passive investor until that point, asked for an explanation. Alex responded, "We have all these potential clients, and I know the connections are going to work. The board will not give me the time I need."

Hassanein believed in the company and knew it was time for action. He made appointments with six target institutions over the course of two days, saying to Alex, "Let's go and see what happens."

In the course of these appointments, Hassanein saw that Alex was brilliant in explaining the company's value proposition and generating a fantastic response from potential clients. Knowing that Alex, given the time he needed, would address the market need and succeed, Hassanein orchestrated the removal of the board. Hassanein raised $8 million, and the company went public with a $250 million IPO less than two years later.

Chances are that along the way, Hassanein made one of his trademark invitations to Alex, "Despite the challenges, there is a better future. Let's work with each other to help it be created."

New Models of Leadership Require Strategic Partnerships, Trust, and Innovation

The best partnerships, according to Hassanein, are strategic ones in which all parties win. He explains:

> *In the case of the Newbridge Networks, the initial strategy was for them to invest in ACC in a way that allowed them to sell the product to their clients at a discounted rate that was preferential to their competitors' rates. From there, the partnership evolved into dedicating funds that would allow us to spin out companies from*

Newbridge—or to invest in companies whose brand name could benefit Newbridge.

Hassanein's role with Newbridge allows him to be developing strategic partnerships continually. Some of today's most innovative companies are involved in personalized medicine or big data analytics for genomes. When Hassanein is looking to secure financing for such companies, he looks for partnerships with companies like Johnson & Johnson, Kaiser Permanente, and Sample Health.

Hassanein seeks out innovation initiatives within the big companies, offering the opportunity to invest in the emerging one. Should the established company choose not to invest, Hassanein explores the possibility of testing the product in partnership with that company. Should the big company agree to product testing, that product's time to the market could be cut by as much as a year-and-a-half. Expenses may be cut by as much as $1.5 million.

Such an arrangement with an established company means the emerging company has a path to growth independent of building a website and launching a marketing campaign. Growth comes from access to the established company's clients, based on the value proposition. If those clients don't like the product from the beginning, the emerging company has the opportunity to ask, "How can we make it such that you would like it?" This type of partnership also provides the established company with an opportunity to potentially buy the emerging one.

Within partnerships, innovation and win/win solutions require new methods of interaction. Partnerships and teams must begin with a foundation of trust as well as new attitudes toward conflict. Traditionally, groups have managed conflict with off-site meetings. In this scenario, differences between individuals become oppositional and metric driven. Somebody wins and somebody loses.

Hassanein is convinced that it's more productive to get together frequently, to focus on discovering new ideas, and then to follow up with consensus. Surprisingly, you can do this via video. Technologies like TelePresence and Google Hangout allow for genuinely open communication. Success comes as team members discover and internalize alternative ideas rather than fighting over them.

One example of a community discovering alternatives involves the brainchild of Naguib Sawiris, Jr. While a young man studying at Stanford, Sawiris came up with a valid platform for home delivery of groceries. The idea is similar to what has become Google Express.

Sawiris' very first client was Walmart, which offered to buy the company for $10 million, just three months after the start of the service. Walmart wrote a letter of intent and told Sawiris that they would confirm their purchase on a certain day. When the day came, the answer was, "No."

Sawiris and his team of seven individuals couldn't see their way forward. Competition was rising, and the company didn't know if they could continue to service Walmart without the buyout. For weeks, the team experienced nothing but misery.

Then, a member of the team came up with an astonishing question and idea. What would happen if they used the platform for a different service? Rather than deliver groceries to homes, what would happen if they used the platform to connect a math teacher to a student?

Less than two months later, the team had a prototype of the new product. In April of 2014, Sawiris became founder and CEO of MathCrunch. Here's an excerpt from a *Forbes Magazine* article published in 2015:

> *The old model of finding a tutor and hiring that person to come to your house once a week no longer makes sense for this generation of students. They often need help immediately, and that's a big part of what attracted*

Miura-Ko to be part of a $3.5 million seed-funding round for MathCrunch. Founded by 23-year-old Naguib Sawiris, MathCrunch is an app that helps students with individual problems on-demand. Tutoring sessions are done entirely through chat. The student sends a photo of the problem that he or she is stuck on, engages with a tutor and then rates the session. Tutors are trained to help guide the student to find the answer. Sessions can last as few as five minutes or as long as an hour.

"Our core belief is that you can build an education service around chat," says Sawiris. "It's what students prefer."

This is an example of an entrepreneur coming up with a good idea, but needing to pivot. The startup had trouble with the market until the team realized that the platform was applicable to multiple markets.

KEY QUESTIONS IN FIVE AREAS
EVERY STARTUP NEEDS TO ANSWER

When talking about entrepreneurship and leading a company forward, Hassanein points to five areas for analysis and questions to ask in each area. He doesn't pretend, however, that the questions are easy to answer.

1. THE IDEA ITSELF
   How do I come up with a good idea and how do I know if the idea I have is good? This is the number one challenge that people face, whether they are at the University of Alexandria or at Stanford.

2. THE TARGET MARKET
   What is the market for this product, and how do I penetrate it? Is the platform or service applicable to more than one market? If the product works in one market, can we license it to another one?

3. THE VALUE PROPOSITION
   What is this product or service's differential value, and how does it stand out?

4. THE TEAM
   What is the right team for this business? What domain knowledge does the team need to succeed? Do the team members have a foundation of trust and the ability to resolve conflict productively?

5. THE NUMBERS
   Where will we spend the money? How much will we get in return?

ADVICE FOR EMERGING LEADERS

1. THINK IN TERMS OF PARTNERSHIP
   Hassanein says, "You may remember Dale Carnegie saying, 'When fate hands you a lemon, make lemonade.' It's always about, What can we do together? Work to create a community of people who work together."

2. WHEN THINGS DON'T WORK,
   FOCUS YOUR ENERGY ON FINDING ALTERNATIVES
   When he recognized that the initial board of ACC was a bad fit, Hassanein understood he had a choice of three responses: submission, confrontation, or alternatives. The only productive solution was to come up with an alternative idea.

3. THINK OF FAILURE AS
   SUCCESS TURNED UPSIDE DOWN
   You can never know how close you are to success. This perspective gives you the strength to keep going rather than giving up.

4. DEVELOP NEW IDEAS AROUND CONFLICT
   Avoid setting up win/lose scenarios such as those built into traditional offsite meetings. Use technology to meet frequently and communicate openly.

Seek to discover and internalize alternative ideas rather than fight over them.

Hassanein has had many pivotal moments in his life and work. These include the one that landed him in jail in Egypt in 1969 and the one that resulted in him becoming CEO of ACC in 1989. In such moments, Hassanein has been committed to seeking new understandings of community, innovation, strategic partnerships, boards of directors, and more. A key reason behind Hassanein's continuing success is summed up in a favorite quote by Marcel Proust: "The journey of life is not about discovering new places, but seeing with new eyes."

SUMMARY

1. Life's pivotal points often come via crises or opportunities in the environment that surrounds us. Hassanein made a job change, in part, because the 1989 San Francisco earthquake made his commute to work unmanageable—a personal crisis in the midst of a much larger one. During that same year, a major opportunity arose when The Department of Defense decided to stop funding work on ARPANET, one of the technologies that became the foundation of the Internet.

2. Hassanein became CEO and Chairman of Advanced Computer Communication (ACC), the company created to capitalize on the opportunity for privatizing ARPANET, successfully raising $40M in investments during a horrible recession.

3. When early sales were 50% lower than projected, the board of directors focused on fault finding rather than adding value. Hassanein realized that this board was a bad fit for the company. After assessing his options, which were to submit, confront, or find alternatives, Hassanein decided to find an alternative, one that allowed the board to dissolved, but in a way they could perceive as a win.

4. He formed a strategic partnership with Sir Terry Matthews, a friend and founder of Newbridge Networks in Ottawa, Canada. Matthews bought out the initial investors and proposed an additional innovation. As a result, Hassanein, in addition to being Chairman of ACC, began to help Newbridge Networks to invest in companies similar to ACC.

5. Hassanein believes that working together as a community is a foundational element of success. All of us, young and old, need a mentor to sit beside us with both head and heart. Hassanein's experience with his own parents exemplifies this sense of support and community.

6. Hassanein's role with Newbridge allows him to be developing strategic partnerships continually. Within partnerships, innovation and win/win solutions require new methods of interaction. Partnerships and teams must begin with a foundation of trust as well as new attitudes toward conflict. He recommends frequent interaction via video technology to focus on discovering new ideas, and then to follow up with consensus. Such interaction can spark innovation and remove the win/lose propositions common in traditional offsite meetings.

7. In any endeavor, Hassanein thinks of failure as success turned upside down. Experience has taught him that you can never know how close you are to success. This perspective provides the strength to keep going rather than giving up.

YOUR NOTES AND REFLECTIONS

_____

_____

_____

_____

_____

_____

_____

_____

_____

Raj Puri
Founder and Chief Executive Officer,
Yanna Technologies

Raj Puri is a technologist and an entrepreneur with a unique blend of technical and business acumen. He has 30-plus years of diverse professional experience, spanning from starting new ventures and creating new products and services, to evangelizing unique business models and launching new international markets. Puri has specialized experience in cybersecurity and compliance matters with business engagements in the United States, Europe, and Asia.

Since 2007, Puri has been actively building and growing Yanna Technologies. Under his leadership, Yanna has become one of the premier names in the areas of cybersecurity, lawful interception, data retention, and mobile investigative services. The company is creating new global standards to innovate around numerous critical issues in these areas.

Puri holds a Bachelor of Science Degree in Electrical & Computer Engineering from the University of Colorado, Boulder, and he has attended various executive leadership and business management courses. He is a frequent speaker and chairperson for numerous groups and conferences, such as Telestrategies, ATIS, ITU, International Engineering Consortium, Supercomm, Institute for International Research, 3GSM Association, and others.

CHAPTER 8

RAJ PURI

Founder and CEO, Raj Puri, interviews every single employee who comes to work at Yanna Technologies, a leading global provider of a wide range of intelligent compliance solutions. Yanna offers customers a cost-effective path to address the complexities related to meeting compliance needs in the rapidly evolving information communications and cloud markets worldwide.

In talking with every potential employee, Puri is not screening or micromanaging the hiring process. If a person is sitting with Puri, he or she has already been interviewed and given a seal of approval.

The conversation Puri has with potential employees is always the same, as it has been for the 200-plus such conversations in the history of Yanna. This conversation is not about technology, although the employees are highly-skilled technology professionals. The conversation is about company culture and a mutual fit. As founder and CEO, Puri has put his indelible stamp on this company, and he believes it's only fair that prospective employees hear about that culture from him. If, in the process, Puri finds the prospective employee doesn't fit the culture, that person doesn't come on board.

In the discussion, Puri tells everyone the three attributes needed to succeed at Yanna. The first is a willingness to work for a nearly anonymous company. Puri speaks of Yanna as a no-name company hidden in Milpitas, California. The company is not a good fit for people who want a flashy, recognizable name like Facebook, Google, or Twitter.

Yanna is a low-profile company that went years without even a website, with ambiguity about what the company did, except for a high-level view. Yanna employees have had to be comfortable with the low profile since the company was founded in 2007. At the same time, Yanna does what Puri calls "crazy, exciting things" for some of the largest organizations and companies. Employees have to be comfortable working with both ambiguity and chaos.

The second attribute leading to success at Yanna is a love for evolution and change. The speed of change is exceptionally fast at Yanna, so much so that what a person has done to date barely matters. The company is currently doing things Puri never thought of in 2007, and just a few years from now, employees will all be doing things they have never done before. Since the company cannot rehire every few years, it needs a staff that embraces change and gladly evolves.

The third attribute is the self-discipline to manage time and execute projects. Yanna is a flat organization. Employees have to manage themselves.

It's not so surprising that these attributes define Puri himself, as well as the culture at Yanna. What's more surprising is Puri's clarity around the culture he has built and needs to maintain in order for the company to accomplish its mission. The pre-employment conversation with every employee is one of the ways Puri creates meaning. Every employee begins at Yanna understanding the organizational culture and its vision, having heard it straight from the Founder and CEO's mouth. Naturally, people remember this conversation.

A Jump into Strategy
Can Take You to the C-Level Suite

Puri didn't have this clarity of vision as he started his career. In fact, he points to one seemingly random decision that set him on an unexpected career trajectory lasting 20-plus years. With a background in engineering and computer science, Puri began his career at NEC Corporation, a provider of telecom and network solutions to business enterprises, communications services providers, and government agencies. One day he received an unsolicited offer to join the consulting firm of Booz Allen Hamilton in Washington D.C.

At the time, Puri had no intention of going into management and/or business strategy, the work that characterizes Booz Allen Hamilton. Puri can't explain why he chose to relocate from Dallas to Washington D.C. to work for Booz Allen Hamilton. He can tell you that this one decision was a pivot point for his entire career.

In retrospect, it seems that Puri just happened to be in the mood for a change. He can now trace a life pattern of major change or shift every seven or eight years. Yanna is in the process of making a major shift even now.

Puri says the change to Booz Allen Hamilton took him completely out of his identity. He had no idea what he was getting into. He didn't have the business school background usually required for this type of job, but he did have experience in the communications market, something Booz Allen Hamilton was beginning to realize it needed.

Booz Allen Hamilton immediately put Puri on a project to work with the U.S. Department of Justice (DOJ) because the company had just gotten one project to do a quick assessment. The DOJ needed to create a strategy in response to a new law affecting the communications market, a new area for Booz Allen Hamilton. Puri began to interact with a variety of government customers and service providers on all sorts of strategy work.

Booz Allen Hamilton recognized that to succeed in the boardroom of high tech companies, they needed team members who had depth in technology, not just MBAs. Puri found himself building a team of nearly 120 communications experts. These experts needed skills that extended beyond engineering. They had to be people who understood technology—

with the ability to work in an ambiguous environment where they could develop and present strategy.

Not only was the new direction a perfect fit for Puri, it has defined everything he has done since. He worked at Booz Allen Hamilton for five years, presenting a variety of products at C-level suites in the United States and Europe. Then Puri began to realize that he not only wanted to develop strategies to give to others, he wanted to build things. In response, he made another jump.

Puri resigned from Booz Allen Hamilton, packed his bags, and drove across the country to the San Francisco Bay area, where he had some friends. He raised about $1 million in angel funding to start MobileRAIN Technologies. Puri relished the challenge of doing something he had never done before—starting something from scratch and raising venture capital. He was excited about what the company could do. Unfortunately, this adventure was cut short by the market crash at the end of February 2001.

With the end of MobileRAIN, Puri went to work for VeriSign, a global leader in domain names and Internet security. At this point, the work Puri had been doing for years began to circle back in a surprising way. A solid business plan and relationships Puri had built in 1995 began to gel in a powerful way early in 2001.

When working at Booz Allen Hamilton, Puri had put together a business plan to bring together a variety of parties, including government agencies and service providers, to work on strategy related to compliance. A company named Illuminet agreed to take ownership of the plan. David Nicol, head of Illuminet's products, agreed to facilitate the initial meeting. All parties loved the plan until, at the last minute, there was a hiccup in who would fund the work. Illuminet did not want to pre-invest into building a business around this plan, and so it did not go forward.

Roughly four years later, Puri emailed a New Years' greeting to David Nicol. In the catch-up conversation that followed, Puri learned that Illuminet had just been acquired by VeriSign. Executives were trying to wrap their arms around communication technologies and make the most of the assets that came with Illuminet. Nicol invited Puri to present the business plan he had presented to Illuminet four years earlier. CEO Stratton Sclavos loved the plan and agreed to fund it. Puri joined VeriSign to launch the NetDiscovery Compliance Service.

The product did well at VeriSign, and the business was expanding. Then, a number of things happened at VeriSign that fundamentally changed the broader business strategy, even though there was a huge market and opportunity for growth. VeriSign changed directions and decided to get rid of a number of assets.

Puri saw his opportunity. He was still interested in the business, and the team was working with interesting key customers and new services. Puri asked if VeriSign minded if he jumped out and started his own company. VeriSign did not mind.

When Puri launched Yanna, mostly from his home, in September 2007, he had one condition for his key customers. They had to pre-fund Yanna for the services because Puri had decided not to raise venture capital.

Yanna grew straight through the recession years that began in 2008, in part, because they had no outside investors. The company works in a unique space in which they've forced customers to come to them.

BUILDING RELATIONSHIPS, TELLING THE STORY, AND MANAGING COMPLEXITY ARE KEY LEADERSHIP BEHAVIORS

The story of Puri's career progression highlights how building and maintaining relationships is an essential leadership behavior. Puri built a business plan at Booz Allen Hamilton in cooperation with people from Illuminet. Years later, Puri launched the product at VeriSign—with the original core of people, only to continue the journey at Yanna years later.

When Puri started Yanna, he was the only ex-VeriSign employee. Now roughly 10 others have joined him there. Puri builds a trusting and loyal relationship with those around him. The key people who surround him today are ones he has known for 20-plus years.

While Puri doesn't think of himself as a born extrovert, he has always nurtured the skill of being able to communicate a story and engage others in that story. For example, while Puri was in high school in Denver, the school got its first computer. Puri and a math teacher figured out how to use the computer and then built a computer science program around it. Puri became an evangelist for the program, presenting it as an opportunity and challenge to his peers. He was practicing putting the pieces together in such a way that others could embrace an opportunity.

At Booz Allen Hamilton, Puri had plenty of chances to refine his skills at presenting in front of industry executives and high-level government officials. Both sides needed to interpret and implement a new law affecting the telecommunications industry. Parties with completely different perspectives needed to agree on a strategy.

An impasse came down to seven items that industry and government could not resolve. On the industry side, executives and technical professionals were saying, "These issues are very complicated. The expectations are unreasonable and it can't be done."

On the government side, people were saying, "This is the law. We have to do it."

Neither side understood the other. They were fighting at a fundamental level and could not see a solution.

Puri and his team took a step back and analyzed the seven issues one by one, seeking out what was reasonable, what was not, and taking up a mediator role.

The small team built a system to clarify the problems. You can think of it as a 1998 version of a simple intuitive video to show how complex things work. The team created a tight system, presentation, and demo, showing it around 50 times from the Attorney General's Office to all the different organizations involved. Once again, Puri was evangelizing an idea and a perspective.

It took about 1½ years for the system to click with the different organizations. Eventually, everyone agreed to five issues rather than seven. They also agreed they could work together on the issues. This is how Puri's team negotiated agreement on the problem so they could begin to work on a solution.

In the work Yanna performs, things are never black and white. Puri and his team members have become skilled at creating meaning for others by speaking to the different perspectives of the different parties involved. They look at both policy and technology, seeking to play in the middle. They broker and mediate solutions, making it seamless and easy for partners to connect.

LIFE IS A JOURNEY, AND LEADERS NEVER GIVE UP

In Buddhism, the word Yanna means a journey, a path, a moving forward. For Puri's life and journey, Churchill's cry, "Never, never, never give up," is a mantra. Somehow, the mantra helps Puri to find the mindset to jump into things with courage. It also gives him the patience needed to stay the course. Puri's journey certainly demonstrates that things don't happen overnight.

Wherever he happens to be on his life journey, Puri is committed to being authentic and integrated. Work life and home life are completely integrated, and there's no room for a false persona at either. Puri says, "I'm not trying to be a CEO or a founder of a company. I'm trying to be who I am. When people try to be someone they are not, they fail."

It's not that Puri doesn't enjoy recognition. He's proud of the fact that Yanna grew from zero employees to 150 during the recession with no investors. He just happens to value authenticity more than rewards. Authenticity is essential to building trusting and loyal relationships.

As a leader and entrepreneur, Puri has faced his share of challenges. One of the toughest came in December of 2014, when Puri was in an accident that caused internal bleeding and required brain surgery. During the recovery, which took roughly six months, Yanna's team, along with Puri's family, stepped up and provided all that was needed. The injury provided a sort of validation for what members of the company were building together. Puri says the event even gave the company a new vigor.

Yanna was in the early stages of making some changes, with great technologies and great customers, when Puri's health was compromised. There was a pause, but things still went forward.

The team held things together, and today the company has a great global sales pipeline. In light of this, Puri is talking to private equity firms to raise money. After a few conversations, Puri is excited about the interest from prestigious firms. Even so, this founder and CEO is cautious. Puri is unwilling to jump quickly until he is confident the potential investor understands Yanna as a company. He wants to forget the numbers until after a discussion about fit.

In describing the process of getting to know an investor, Puri mentions the interview he has with every potential employee. The same fundamental principle applies here. An investor has to understand how Yanna was built, how it works with customers, and what the company values before there can be a relationship. If the fit isn't there, the relationship doesn't happen.

Puri is interviewing potential investors for fit before he decides to accept their money or not. That's a real commitment to alignment and integrity.

ADVICE TO EMERGING LEADERS

Puri's life journey and approach to his company's culture demonstrates clear lessons to emerging leaders:

1. WHEN LOOKING FOR A JOB,
   PAY ATTENTION TO CULTURE AS WELL AS THE JOB
   While technology and other work attributes are important, a mismatch between employee and culture negatively affects both.

   When choosing a company to invest your life in, ask questions about culture. When interviewing candidates to become members of your team, tell them about your culture and make sure you have a good fit.

2. EMBRACE EVOLUTION AND CHANGE
   While the speed of change is especially fast at Yanna, it is fast everywhere. No one can rely on job skills or experience he or she has perfected in the past. The ability to contribute effectively depends on an attitude that embraces change and willingness to continually learn and grow.

3. SPEAK TO DIFFERENT
   PERSPECTIVES OF DIFFERENT PARTIES
   A significant portion of Yanna's success is the team's ability to productively address a variety of perspectives and stakeholders. They look at both policy and technology, seeking to play in the middle. They broker and mediate solutions, making it seamless and easy for partners to connect.

4. BE WHO YOU ARE
   Puri is personally committed to living an authentic and integrated life. For him, work and home life are all a part of the whole, and there is no room to be a false persona in either place. He says, "I'm not trying to be a CEO or a founder of a company. I'm try-

ing to be who I am. When people try to be someone they are not, they fail."

5. NEVER GIVE UP

Puri's journey demonstrates that success doesn't typically happen overnight. Puri takes Winston Churchill's cry, "Never, never, never give up," as a mantra. The mantra helps Puri to find the mindset to jump into things with courage as well as to find the patience he needs to stay the course.

SUMMARY

1. Founder and CEO Raj Puri interviews every employee who comes to work at Yanna Technologies, not with the intent to micromanage, but to ensure a good cultural fit. As founder and CEO, Puri has put his indelible stamp on Yanna, and he believes it is appropriate for prospective employees to hear about that culture from him.

2. In Buddhism, the word Yanna means a journey, a path, a moving forward.

3. At Yanna, a good fit includes three attributes: willingness to work for a low-profile company; a love for evolution and change; and an ability to manage time and execute projects in a flat organization.

4. Puri's own willingness to embrace change caused him to accept a job offer that shifted his career and put him on the trajectory that led to Yanna Technologies. With a background in engineering and computer science, Puri began his career at NEC Corporation, a provider of telecom and network solutions to business enterprises, communications services providers, and government agencies. One day he received an unsolicited offer to join the consulting firm of Booz Allen Hamilton in Washington D.C. This change led him to enter the arenas of management and strategy.

5. The story of Puri's career progression highlights how building and maintaining relationships is an essential leadership behavior. Puri built a business plan at Booz Allen Hamilton in cooperation with people from Illuminet. Years later, Puri launched the product at VeriSign —with the original core of people—only to continue the journey at Yanna years later.

6. In the work Yanna performs, things are never black and white. Yanna is successful, in part, because Puri and his team members are skilled at creating meaning for others by speaking to the different perspectives of the different

parties involved. They broker and mediate solutions, making it seamless and easy for partners to connect.

7. Personally, Puri has a commitment to living an authentic and integrated life. He believes that people who try to be something they are not will fail.

YOUR NOTES AND REFLECTIONS

_____

_____

_____

_____

_____

_____

_____

_____

_____

_____

_____

_____

_____

DAVID MARTIN
President and Chief Executive Officer,
Cardiovascular Systems, Inc.

Martin joined Cardiovascular Systems, Inc. (CSI) as a director in 2006 and became CEO of the New Brighton-based company in 2007. CSI makes diamond-encrusted medical devices that clear out clogged arteries.

Martin led the business through a major expansion into the coronary artery disease market, a long-time goal of the company's founders. During Martin's tenure, CSI grew from a pre-revenue startup organization to a public company with fiscal year 2015 revenues in excess of $180 million with two unique, high-margin applications addressing vascular disease.

Martin started his career as a salesperson pitching Metamucil to gastroenterologists. He went on to hold leadership roles at several med-tech companies, including the COO position at Fox-Hollow Technologies, Inc.

He received a Bachelor of Arts degree from the University of California at Santa Barbara and a Master of Business Administration degree at the University of San Diego.

Unfortunately, Martin passed away during the writing of this book (May 1, 2016). We are grateful for all that he contributed to the book and the medical device industry. We have kept present tense in this chapter, relating David's experience as he described it to us during the interview.

CHAPTER 9

DAVID MARTIN

When David Martin took the helm as CEO at the fledgling company, Cardiovascular Systems, Inc. (CSI), his expectations of the job were a world away from what the job turned out to be. CSI is a medical device company that makes and sells devices for removing plaque from arteries. David's role, beginning as a board member in 2006, was to take the firm from a private company with no product approval for its device, to a company with approval to sell in the United States, with the revenue and proof of corporate benefit to take the company public.

Martin was brought in to strategize, raise money, hire, and then execute the plan to take CSI public. By 2008, Martin was CEO, and CSI was queued up and ready to make the move. Martin was confident, having been a member of three different teams that had taken companies public. Each had a successful device that contributed to patients and made great commercial stories.

Martin explains the situation with CSI this way:

Everything seemed great. The market, the people, the investment banking, and the process for getting the device approved all were working. It seemed like a smooth path to success.

In 2008, CSI was lined up with an S1 [SEC filing for a company intending to go public] and a great slate of bankers, including Morgan Stanley, for going public. This company was behaving in a way with product approvals, milestone achievement, and revenue that none

*of the previous three companies had, so this one was re-
ally shaping up to be a gold standard that year for a
medical device*

*As the year emerged, the volatility index, as we all know
now, started going up and down. People were wondering what was happening, and the crash was starting to
affect us. Small, private companies don't have big bank
loads, so as the months and quarters went on, things began to go wrong, including the banking shake up. We
lost our top tier banker, and suddenly we were past the
target date for financing.*

In retrospect, the crash had a defined timeline, but as it
emerged, no one had the ability to foresee this. The path ahead
that had appeared easy and smooth to Martin a mere two years
earlier was now full of mud and obstacles. Rather than the job
Martin had signed on for, moving the company forward, he
was faced with the leadership challenge of trying to survive
during the crash.

Martin remembers the crisis of being down to one payroll,
the pressure that came with that, and the uncertainty of what
was on the road ahead. Healthcare is capital intensive, and the
leadership team could not know how long the financing crisis
would last. In the absence of knowing what was going to happen, they had to decide how to respond.

Martin, along with his board, defined their jobs as preserving choices and surviving as a company.

LEADERS SUSTAIN DRIVE IN ROUGH TIMES

When asked how he found the drive to keep going, Martin
first credits his own, along with the CSI boards', fundamental
belief in the technology.

The leadership team knew the device that CSI was working on would satisfy a large and unmet need. They had seen
what the device could do for patients who were at end stage

vascular disease. They had seen the response from physicians who treated these patients. They had seen people scheduled for amputation be treated with their device and ultimately walk out of the hospital.

Coupled with that fundamental belief was an appreciation for an economic cycle. Martin says:

Capitalism isn't pretty. It is a series of ups and downs. What I had learned previously, that helped me through that season, was that there are ups and downs; there are open windows and closed windows. There are open and closed windows in financing, as well as epic IPO years and down years. I had an appreciation of economic downturns and upswings, so preserving was the right thing to do for the leadership team.

Fortunately, CSI had a board of mature directors who had been there and done that.

Directors had experience with many companies with great products. The chair, who was approaching his 70s, had extensive experience both in healthcare and financing. Martin believes the experience of the board was a key factor in the company's survival.

On the executive team, Martin gives credit to a couple of anchors. The team included a CFO who was "gray haired and experienced" and moving into the role of Chief Administrative Officer. Martin had just hired a new CFO, who later earned the nickname, Iron, because he is iron-like.

All told, Martin had literally 40 years of public company key financial officer experience sitting there during the crisis. Those people are still with CSI today.

AUTHENTIC COMMUNICATION
LEADS TO LEADERSHIP SUCCESS

The leadership team sought to practice message consistency. They believed the key was to express fundamental belief for the opportunity and the commitment that goes along with that, without sugarcoating the environment.

Employees were fearful. They had been expecting CSI to transition from a small company to a big one. Many employees were worried about their next paycheck. Martin says:

> We were just honest. We didn't make any promises we couldn't keep, but we communicated, and I think that is what it takes. It's important to communicate formally and informally, in groups and one-on-one. It is not hard to do this when you have fewer than 50 employees— that's what we did and it worked. We needed to answer employee's questions: Will I get a paycheck? Will the company still be up for investors? Will the company survive?

Martin was committed to communicating with every audience: directors, executive team, employees, investors, physician partners, etc. Each audience involved challenging conversations. For example, some of CSI's top engineers said, "Hey, I've got kids and I'm uncertain about what's going to happen here. I have an opportunity to work with a big company. If I go over there, I know they will never tell me I can't get a paycheck. I can't say that if I stay here."

Martin was honest about cash being tight and that a missed payroll could happen at CSI. He could only tell the employees that he was committed and describe the steps the company was taking. Martin says:

> In those conversations, you have to let people do what is right for them, so we lost some engineering talent to some of the big companies at that time. But because of the candor, I think we won a lot of people who would have otherwise walked out the door. They liked being in the know; they embraced the challenge and accepted the risk. In the end, they became part of the CSI lore and story of success. They were fulfilled about the choice

they made given the facts, so the employee loyalty was unbelievable.

One critical conversation was the pivotal point for everything that followed. Martin met with one of his bankers from Morgan Stanley, who had just gotten the news that he was being let go as part of a downsizing.

While some venture capitalists cast a wary eye on the investment banker and vice versa, Martin doesn't see anyone as an adversary. From his perspective, partners and investment bankers offer a great service. You have to build trust and form a partnership with the people you work with.

After the banker told Martin the bad news about him leaving Morgan Stanley, the two still met. When Martin revealed that CSI was down to a couple of payrolls in cash, the banker had an idea. In a meeting at Morgan Stanley, the banker had encountered a company called Replidyne that had cash and a product that had just gone sideways with the FDA.

Replidyne was staring down the pipe of seven more years, expecting to chew up dollars before they could resubmit. Although he no longer worked for Morgan Stanley, the banker informed the leadership at Replidyne that he believed there was a match with a little company in Minnesota called CSI.

Doubtful, they responded that Replidyne had already talked to 90 companies. The banker explained that CSI had a project and no money while their company had money and no project.

Martin and his team pitched to a couple of the Replidyne board members over the phone and then were invited to pitch at a live meeting. This invitation came, even though CSI was the last of nearly 100 companies Replidyne had explored as they searched for a match.

The live pitch turned out to be a big success, winning the $30-plus million CSI needed to bridge from one place to another.

That live pitch was a key meeting, leading to additional key meetings within the company. CSI had planned on a $75-plus million dollar IPO and intended to fuel a plan requiring $75 million. Given that they now had only $30 million, they had to make adjustments.

The next series of meetings at the company was about how to match an operating plan to the money available and still service as many patients as possible. CSI, with its vascular device, was founded on the opportunity to save patients with coronary artery disease.

One of the key decisions was to seek FDA approval for use of the CSI device in the legs only. This would be an easier, shorter, and less expensive route than the one originally planned. There were a number of meetings relative to this, but Martin remembers an early one with Larry Betterley, his relatively new CFO.

When Martin hired Betterley, a best in class CFO, CSI had already chosen the bankers, and the S1 was 80 percent developed. In the interview process, Martin told Betterley, "This one is set, it is going, it is a piece of cake, and you just need to get on board."

Martin sincerely believed this at the time. Yet, four or five weeks into Betterley's employment, the bad news started to come in. Suddenly, Betterley had a different task than he expected—but so did everyone else. It turns out Betterley responded well to the situation, and he and Martin formed a great relationship. Betterley is still a critical member of the executive team.

Effective Leaders Focus on Their Top Responsibilities

As CEO, Martin felt a deep responsibility for two things as he led the company through the crisis. First, he felt a responsibility to his teammates and their families. He appreciated the people, their contributions, and their personal responsibilities.

Martin also felt a profound responsibility to serve the opportunity. People who work in the healthcare and medical device fields can love their jobs because they serve an opportunity that begins with a disease state. They have a chance to work together to solve complex problems to improve people's health.

Despite the attraction of working on a vascular cure that would save lives, Martin hadn't anticipated being underfunded for a long and uncertain time. He was surprised to discover that his responsibility to others and the opportunity to make a difference in the lives of others made being a CEO and team member fulfilling. His twin responsibilities seemed to cement something that Martin had perhaps practiced before without thinking much about it.

When Martin joined CSI as a board member in 2006, it seemed like the process of going public was teed up; the company might be birthed and done in a period of 36 months. When reality was the opposite of that—36 months of pain—it turned out that Martin liked it. He discovered that serving the opportunity is fun and provides a great experience in teamwork.

LEADERS EMBRACE AND GROW FROM POSITIVE ROLE MODELS

When asked about positive influences that helped shape his leadership perspective, Martin mentions a successful CEO and venture capitalist who served as an early mentor. This CEO, the person in charge of an early private-to-public offering in Martin's career, demonstrated open communication and workplace efficiency by walking around the operation. The CEO didn't mind if someone overheard what he said during his walks. And if someone chose to ask about the operating plan or any area of the business, he was willing to answer. Martin says:

You felt very much like you were on a team; like you were included. The CEO empowered others. As an employee working in that environment, I was willing to work the 18-hour day, travel on weekends, and go the extra mile. I cared; I wanted to win. That open society which comes with understanding that we are working together was great, and the chance to be recognized, solve a problem, and be appreciated for it was highly motivating.

Years later, when Martin joined CSI, he believed he was an established leader. It turns out he still had a lot to learn. He says:

I remember the influence of one particular board member, John Freeman, during a crucial conversation. When the CSI board met and talked about Replidyne's offer and the conditions, as can happen, people wanted to win with negotiation. Replidyne wanted two board seats rather than the standard one seat, and this was a concern. Freeman went the extra mile and did enough research to know that Replidyne actually had two really good board members to offer.

In the moment of crisis, everyone was taking an "us against them" position and didn't want to comply with the condition. Freeman broke that tie by saying, "Look, we could probably use some more intellect here. I know one of the people who is interested; the other one has a great reputation." John's perspective carried the day.

The group was also struggling with percentages of ownership. Everyone on the CSI board was digging in until Freeman said, "Do you realize we are talking about a fraction of 1 percent?" Suddenly, that struggle no longer seemed so important. And the deal got done.

Martin noticed and appreciated what John did—because Martin would not have done it. He says, "I learned from that moment that digging in on one detail at the expense of the overall win is not always the right thing to do."

Another mentor was then Chairman of CSI, the late Glen Nelson. Nelson had a long and distinguished career in both business and medicine. Nelson was first a physician, a surgeon for 20 years, running a large practice. He stepped into the medical device industry through Medtronic and made a series of decisions and acquisitions that grew that company from startup to tens of billions of dollars, and all of the contribution that goes with that.

Nelson was wise and unflappable. When the crash came, it would have been easy to take a short-term approach with the small company. CSI might have focused on what the dollar would get them right then or what they could accomplish in 90 days or 180 days. As chairman, Glen Nelson made sure the company had vision and a long-term look at every decision they made. Because of that, CSI built a solid platform for itself and went forward to save and serve a quarter of a million patients at end stage vascular disease—so far.

Martin's experience at CSI, especially under the influence of Freeman and Nelson, sparked profound change in his leadership style. In 2006, he fit the profile of a brash and confident professional from Silicon Valley, who had a deep understanding of how startup companies work and how to bring a company from private to public, build good teams, and reach milestones. The CSI board, located in Minnesota, sought someone to fit that profile and found Martin, even though they hadn't known his name.

At first, Martin said no to the CEO job, but he agreed to join the board. He describes what happened next:

I became CEO six months later. I'm different now. I think I appreciate the contributions of others more now than ever. I always relished in the team play and the camaraderie that came with working at these startups. The work is so hard; your experience involves some suffering and failure; but you also enjoy the success. I always loved that; it drove me, but now I'd like to think that I've incorporated a lot of Glen Nelson and the long-term view.

I'd like to think I have even more appreciation for people and their commitments and the things a leader can do to support them. People are motivated when they become part of the problem solving and contribute to achieving the milestones. People make the difference; they always do. I think that as every year goes by (there have been 10 since I've been the CEO of CSI), that one truth hits me hard and hits me often, that it is the people that matter. I think that is the biggest one for me. It just gets bolder.

"People make a difference" has become a mantra for me, something I say every time I am speaking to team members or toasting success. Thanking people for their contribution and their partnership is the most important thing. We need other things, of course, like quality metrics and statements on the wall, but recognizing people is the big one for me.

Looking back, Martin realizes just how much he did not know when he took over the helm at CSI. He has much more experience now, but in any situation, he is aware that he doesn't know it all. He is always looking for the Larry Betterley, Glen Nelson, or John Freeman who can provide insight and wisdom. Martin says, "You have to appreciate that you probably don't have it all. You can bring a lot and you should, but if you are not open to solutions from other people you are probably not going to do great things."

GOOD LEADERSHIP AND GOOD COMMUNICATION ARE INTRICATELY CONNECTED

Martin believes there is a direct correlation between commitment and communication, so he has learned to communicate formally and informally with all groups of stakeholders. He creates a schedule and works to keep to that schedule. For example, Martin meets with his executive team as a group each week and informally throughout the week.

Martin appreciates the value of group meetings, but he knows that everyone also needs one-on-one time. He believes a leader must formalize the one-on-one meeting process, knowing that if you let the communication go, your opportunity will suffer. You are less able to serve the opportunity. Looking back over the course of his 10 years as CEO, Martin sees that when his discipline surrounding communication lapsed, even for a legitimate reason, the opportunity suffered. Today, he works to pace himself and stay consistent.

Martin embraces the need to communicate with external audiences as well as internal ones. He takes the perspective that "the investors are always your friends and your allies; they are never the enemy; and they will partner with you to serve the opportunity." Communication with investors, as well as with the company's board, needs to be frequent. It's a mistake to wait for scheduled board meetings. A CEO needs to communicate with board members often, not necessarily in lengthy conversations. "You've got to give them the pearls; you've got to give them a little bit of metrics and a little bit of insight—and you've got to do that with frequency."

As CEO, Martin has always tried to err on the side of over communication, even as the executive team layered information down through the company. At a small medical device company, leaders need to go deep with communication because people need to solve really complex problems.

Martin asks his executive team members to communicate weekly with their teams, after the weekly executive team meeting. As the communication filters down, people don't need to know every issue or every detail, but they do need information. Martin encourages his leadership team to schedule time to walk around and to take employees out to lunch to hear about what they are working on.

Each group of stakeholders has to feel informed and included. In the medical device field, the group includes physician partners, employees, investors, directors, and even the government agencies. It may be tempting to complain about government agencies, but that doesn't serve the opportunity. To succeed, you have to build partnerships with all stakeholders.

ADVICE TO EMERGING LEADERS

Asked to share leadership advice with emerging leaders, Martin makes two suggestions:

1. GET EVERYONE ON BOARD
   TO SERVE THE OPPORTUNITY
   If you don't keep people focused on serving the opportunity, they will work at cross-purposes. When people feel they are solving problems in order to help people, their energy points in the right direction.

2. TAKE AN ACTIVE INTEREST IN OTHERS
   In Martin's industry, this might involve taking an interest in the world of vascular surgeons, cardiologists, and universal radiologists. These doctors have a tough job. Dealing with endless rules and regulations while trying to develop a practice and pay back years of debt is not easy.

   Many problems can be solved by taking an active interest in others, and the relationships you build count in good times and bad times. In the medical device field, for example, there are inspections to pass, and a myriad of bureaucracy. Communicating across disciplines and departments, appreciating others' work and expertise is critical.

Reflecting on Martin's development as a leader over the past 10-plus years, it is clear that the great crisis he experienced at CSI in 2008 was an opportunity as well as a huge test. The crash provided a situation in which Martin could not simply forge ahead with the methods he had used in his three previous startups. One of Martin's greatest achievements was listening to, and learning from, seasoned and mature board members and executives. This action, which must have been challenging for a young and brash CEO, broadened his perspective and built strong partnerships inside and outside of CSI. The act of listening and respecting the experience of others allowed Martin to serve his team members and the opportunity to improve—and even save—the lives of those struggling with end stage vascular disease.

SUMMARY

1. David Martin originally signed on at CSI to take the firm from a private company with no product approval for its medical device, to a company with approval to sell in the United States, with the revenue and proof of corporate benefit to take the company public. All indicators were positive until the company lost its top tier bank in the 2008 crash. Martin's job changed from taking the company public to steering its survival during the crash.

2. Martin and his leadership team had confidence in the product and opportunity it offered to patients with end stage vascular disease. That, coupled with an understanding of economic cycles, gave them the drive needed to keep going. The team committed to consistently communicating the opportunity, without sugarcoating what was going on in the environment.

3. With fewer than 50 employees at the time, they were able to communicate formally and informally, to address employees' questions and fears honestly. Some left for fear of the company missing payroll; those who stayed became especially loyal to the mission of the company.

4. CSI successfully pitched to Replidyne, a company that had cash and a product that had just gone sideways with the FDA. This gave them the cash they needed to go forward with their IPO, although in a more limited fashion than originally intended.

5. Martin credits Chairman of the Board, Glen Nelson, with ensuring the company had vision and a long-term look at every decision they made. Because of this, CSI built a solid platform for itself and went forward to save and serve a quarter of a million patients at end stage vascular disease—so far.

6. The experience with Nelson and other mentors at CSI changed Martin's approach to leadership. Martin has come to appreciate the contributions of people more and

to look for the wisdom of others. He says, "You have to appreciate that you probably don't have it all. You can bring a lot and you should, but if you are not open to solutions from other people you are probably not going to do great things."

7. Believing there is a direct correlation between commit-ment and communication, Martin has learned to com-municate formally and informally with all groups of stakeholders and encourages his leadership team to do the same. He looks at all stakeholders, even investors and regulators, as allies. Looking back over the course of his 10 years as CEO, Martin noticed that when his discipline surrounding communication lapsed, even for a legitimate reason, the opportunity suffered.

YOUR NOTES AND REFLECTIONS

_____

_____

_____

_____

_____

_____

_____

_____

_____

_____

_____

_____

_____

_____

_____

_____

_____

_____

_____

_____

_____

_____

_____

SUZANNE EVANS
Founder and Owner
Susanne Evans Coaching, LLC

Suzanne Evans, went from secretary to a 6 million dollar business in just six years. Her company landed in the INC 500/5000 for four straight years and she lost 75 pounds in the process.

Suzanne Evans has become the "Tell it like it is," no fluff boss of business building. As founder and owner of Suzanne Evans Coaching, LLC, she went from secretary to surpassing the seven-figure mark in just over three years. Today, Evans supports, coaches, and teaches over 30,000 women enrolled in her wealth and business building programs. She says, "Turning my 'mess into my message' helped me quickly build a seven-figure business. Then something funny happened: Other entrepreneurs wanted to know how I did it. It's why in 2008, I started a company designed to help people make millions while making a difference."

Evans launched four businesses in four months, making hundreds of thousands of dollars. Refusing to shy away from confrontation or "play by the rules," she quickly earned a reputation for being a bit "in your face," contrasting with many other coaches who take a softer approach.

Evans, who was educated at New York University, is founder and benefactor of Help More People Foundation.

.

CHAPTER 10

SUZANNE EVANS

One day in 2007, Suzanne Evans performed some calculations. As a result, she realized that, if she continued to work her day job on Broadway, it would take 21 years to pay off her debts. With this realization came a moment of decision. Evans describes it this way:

I could "live smaller" and be afraid of money and wealth, or I could find a way to double my income. I knew my day job (which, frankly, after 10 years had left me unsatisfied) would never give me the lifestyle I needed to become the person I always knew I could be. I wanted to make a mark, I wanted to leave a legacy, and though I didn't know what to do, what I did know was that I had to do something, and quick.

Evans decided to start her own business. Reflecting on her gifts, talents, and what she calls "my mess," Evans recognized that she was great at helping people. She pursued certification as a life coach and opened her door for business.

When prospects didn't immediately beat down her door, Evans realized that to succeed, she would have to master marketing and sales. She also realized that she needed to find a way to turn her own "mess" into a serious business to help other people.

Turning her "mess into my message" helped Evans quickly build a seven-figure business. Other entrepreneurs soon wanted to know Evans' path and secrets for success. They were ready to pay Evans to teach them. In 2008, she started

Help More People, a company designed to help people earn millions while making a difference.

The goal was simple: Help women entrepreneurs get rid of their shame around money, marketing and sales, so they could build businesses that leave a legacy while making a fortune.

With just three years in business, Evans went from secretary to surpassing the seven-figure mark. Today, she and her team support, coach, and teach over 30,000 women enrolled in the company's wealth and business building programs. Recent accomplishments include the following:

- Coaching private clients to total revenues exceeding 25 million dollars

- Creating the Be the Change Award for business owners making a difference

- Launching the Give Movement, a not-for-profit serving women worldwide in education, entrepreneurship, and equality

LEADERSHIP IS ABOUT MANAGING THE GAME

When asked to describe a pivotal opportunity or crisis in her own professional life, Evans doesn't mention the decision point that led her to start her own business. In fact, Evans doesn't think about business in terms of pivotal moments. Rather, she thinks that every day in business presents its own crisis. Business, in Evans' view, is a game you play every day, one that requires you to understand the rules and the players. The game requires you to be able to change the rules and remain standing, no matter what comes your way.

People not thinking of business this way may not be attending sufficiently to cash flow, managing their money effectively, or treating their employees well. This lack of attention and care can bring on self-imposed crises.

While there are crises that come from external sources, like natural disasters and terrorism, these are not events you can control. Leaders can control what they do every day. All effective leaders sit in rooms figuring out cash flow and worrying that the stocks are going to fall. There may not be a lot of glamor in this, but all the best business leaders pay careful attention to daily realities.

Evans says, "Here's the bottom line: Business leadership is about waking up every day and being someone who can handle crisis control. You develop the ability to water a garden to keep it growing in one area of the business while fighting a fire in a different area." It becomes a balance of emotional fortitude.

Evans uses a number of images to describe her understanding of the nature of business and leadership. These include sun, water, and the reality show, *Survivor*.

The image of the sun describes the basic attitude Evans embraced at a young age after watching her father. Her dad demonstrated a steady awareness that the sun would rise every morning and set every night. He habitually let go of the things he could not control and focused on the things he could control. Evans' mother had the opposite habit. She worried about the sun rising, setting, and everything that might happen in between.

Evans subscribes to her father's view. Appreciating the difference between what you can control and what you can't is a path to peace. Evans believes that most of the success in managing and running a business comes with knowing that everything is in the present moment. It comes with knowing there will be a next moment and one more after that.

Given that Evans now lives near the water, the ebb and flow of the tide is a daily reminder that business is an ebb and flow of success and failure. Employees come and go. Leaders need to expect expansion and contraction. They need to be good surfers who can go the distance.

The ability to be the last one standing, of course, is what the reality show, *Survivor*, is all about. The winner is the one who can outwit, outlast, and outplay the others. The final fate of a contestant does not rest on the biggest crisis faced, but on how he or she handles the game in all of the days between the crises. The same is true in business. You will win some challenges and lose some. What matters is that you keep playing the game. She says:

> *It's not necessarily the smartest, most creative, or most interesting business leader who succeeds. The one who succeeds is the one who has the ability to be the last person standing.*

LEADERSHIP IS MORE ABOUT HONESTY THAN FRAMING MESSAGES

Many leaders work to frame issues so that employees will view them in certain ways. Evans is not among them. As someone who gives speeches for a living, Evans likes to talk—but she has learned that shutting up can be more productive. A habit of listening leads to a flow of priceless information.

Evans believes in honesty and over communicating with employees. She presents the facts to employees and then asks, "What do you think this means? What does this mean for you? What does this mean for me?" She tries to lay all the cards on the table and then let her team members bring forth what it looks like to them or what their experience is. Only after carefully listening does Evans respond, "Let me tell you what it means for me—and what I see it means for us."

Evans used this approach when an important manager in her company was let go, and Evans needed to figure out what to do next. Being adamant that every issue deserves a dialogue, she asked employees what the change meant for them emotionally, professionally, and managerially. Evans is careful to explain that this was a facilitated dialogue rather than a democracy. "A dialogue informs decision-making. In a democracy, nothing gets done. You can't run a business that way."

Evans believes that open dialogues allow you to uncover the most effective next steps. Managers and business owners spend quite a bit of time assuming what people need and want and imposing on them what the managers want them to do and be. Certainly, leaders need to have a vision for the company and metrics to judge performance, but at some point, "you can't make a Doberman a poodle."

Conversations, in which leaders ask employees what they are experiencing, what they need, and what a change means for them, can lead to surprising intelligence. In fact, in the instance in which an important manager was let go, Evans learned that she didn't need to replace that person. Without the open conversations, she doubts that she would have discovered that. To miss that intelligence would have been expensive from a salary perspective, a management perspective, and an emotional perspective.

For Evans' team of 30-plus, open dialogues occur in the context of regular communication about company vision, goals, and metrics. The whole team carves out time to meet a few times a year so that individuals will understand where the company is headed, what's expected of them, and what role they play in the overall operation.

For the sales team, the conversations occur weekly. Together, the sales team sets goals, establishes metrics, and positions itself to meet those metrics. It's critical that all team members know what is expected of them personally and as a department. Experience tells Evans that it's unwise to assume employees can set their own metrics effectively. She has often seen employees submit sales quotas that are too high, setting themselves up for failure.

Speaking of her sales team, Evans repeats her belief in the value of over communicating. This doesn't mean leaders have to constantly host physical meetings. Technology allows for frequent communication. For example, members of Evan's sales team frequently send group texts to keep everyone informed about where they are in terms of goals and metrics. This allows everyone to easily stay up-to-date on where performance stands against goals and metrics.

Leadership Involves Three Key Behaviors

When asked to explain the key values or skills that describe Evans' leadership philosophy or style, Evans replies with concepts that can be described in three words: consistency, forgiveness, and modeling.

Evans strives for a workplace in which surprises are the exception rather than the norm, because consistency is crucial to good leadership. Evans consistently expresses disappointment in certain things and consistently rewards others. She is consistent in calling out when something isn't done right or well.

On the other hand, Evans is quick to forgive. While she will lay down the line about something that isn't done well, she won't hold a grudge about it. She does not hold onto people's performance in a personal way.

In demonstrating a quickness to forgive, Evans builds an emotional connection with her employees. She is proud to say that of the employees who have chosen to leave the company, a high percentage have come back or currently work with the company in some capacity. Evans stays in touch and supports people who have worked with her. The fact that the support goes both ways says a lot about the nature of the company. This doesn't mean Evans is a soft boss; in fact, she has a reputation for being demanding and being clear on expectations. Her team works hard and plays hard.

For Evans, a third key is modeling the behavior she wants to see in the company. She remembers a basketball coach who told team members, "I will never ask you to run a suicide run that I wouldn't run." In similar manner, Evans earns respect by pitching in. She says, "If there is a stain on the carpet and everyone is struggling, I'll be one of the first ones to get down and take a turn." A leader can't get respect by demanding it, but she can earn it by showing people that she is willing to help and work at whatever level everyone else is working.

BUILDING A BUSINESS MEANS RELEASING OTHERS TO SUCCEED

Starting out, Evans named her company Suzanne Evans Coaching, LLC. She was the brand, the coach, the success story, and the vision for the company. Eight years later, her photo is still front and center on the website. Evans' vision of the company, however, has evolved. Today, Evans envisions a company that is less and less about Suzanne Evans—and more able to survive should something happen to its founder.

The company is in a transition period and has plans to rebrand as Hell Yeah, Inc. This name reflects the bold, in-your-face style Evans is known for. In fact, one company web page begins by inviting prospects to answer "Hell Yeah" to all four of the following questions:

- Want to make more money?
- Ready to find your movement?
- Want to grow your business?
- Ready to change your life?

Evans acknowledges that many business owners try to hold on to center stage—with a business model that withholds information and control. In Evans' view, this model leads to mistrust and fear in the minds of employees. And nothing is worse than an employee who is afraid because he or she doesn't understand what's happening and feels insecure in the job. In such situations, the owner or highest-level managers typically do the majority of the work. There are a lot of assistants and a little bit of leadership. Such a company may be moderately successful, but it will be miserable to work for and to run.

Evans' business model is built on many leadership roles, with a few assistants supporting those roles. The company is divided into divisions, or pods, with managers each running his or her own division. The company has a Private Coaching pod, a Hell Yeah Mastery pod, a Hell Yeah Studios pod, and a Marketing pod. While some things in the company are still dependent on Evans, the goal is to ensure the divisions are managed in such a way that each could spin off and run by itself or be sold.

The secret to success with this business model—as in every aspect of managing the business—is to over communicate. Only when an owner shares what is going on in the company can an employee be part of that company and give his or her best. Over communication is at the heart of trust, and at the heart of success. Evans says, "No one in the history of this company has ever come up to me and said, 'You know, you are over communicating to me.' That's never going to happen, right?"

ADVICE TO EMERGING LEADERS

Evans' story and business model all speak loudly to emerging leaders. Here are a few highlights:

1. CHOOSE TO LIVE BIG RATHER THAN SMALL
   Say, "Hell Yeah!"

2. DON'T BE AFRAID OR ASHAMED
   In the midst of your "mess," find your talents and embrace them. Get rid of any shame you may have around money, marketing, or sales.

3. APPRECIATE THE DIFFERENCE BETWEEN WHAT YOU CAN CONTROL AND WHAT YOU CAN'T
   While you may not be able to control crises from external sources or business cycles, you can control what you do every day. Discipline yourself to pay

attention to the daily realities of business, such as cash flow and money management. Pay constant attention to how you treat employees.

4. BUILD EMOTIONAL CONNECTIONS WITH EMPLOYEES
This doesn't mean you have to be a soft boss, simply that you support the people who work for you.

5. CULTIVATE HABITS OF
OVER COMMUNICATING AND LISTENING
Communicate facts honestly and ask employees what those facts mean to them. Foster dialogues, listen, and learn from what you hear. The information your employees share is priceless.

6. HELP OTHERS SUCCEED
Share center stage with others, and develop leaders rather than assistants. Give employees the information they need to step up and give their best. That's the only way they can truly belong to an organization.

SUMMARY

1. Turning her "mess into my message" helped Evans quickly build a seven-figure business. Other entrepreneurs soon wanted to know Evans' path and secrets for success. They were ready to pay Evans to teach them. In 2008, she started Help More People, a company designed to help people earn millions while making a difference. Today the company is rebranding as Hell Yeah, Inc. This name reflects the bold, in-your-face style Evans is known for.

2. Rather than think about pivotal points of crisis or opportunity, Evans thinks every business day represents a crisis of its own. The thing that matters most is how the leader manages each day between bigger crises. To be an effective leader, you must pay careful attention to daily realities.

3. From her father, Evans learned that appreciating the difference between what you can control and what you can't is a path to peace. From this perspective, most of the success in managing and running a business comes with knowing that everything is in the present moment—and knowing there will be a next moment and one more after that.

4. Evans believes in honesty and over communicating with employees. She presents the facts to employees and then asks, "What do you think this means? What does this mean for you? What does this mean for me?" She is adamant that every issue deserves a dialogue and that a leader learns a great deal by listening. This does not mean Evans is running a democracy, simply that dialogue informs decision-making.

5. Three words describe this business owner's leadership style: consistency, forgiveness, and modeling. She believes in consistently expressing disappointment in certain things and consistently rewarding others. While she will lay down the line about something that isn't done well,

Evans will not hold a grudge about it. She does not hold onto people's performance in a personal way. Evans earns respect by modeling a willingness to work at the same level as everyone else.

6. Evans builds an emotional connection with her employees. She stays in touch and supports people who have worked with her in the past. The fact that the support goes both ways says a lot about the nature of her company. This doesn't mean Evans is a soft boss; in fact, she has a reputation for being demanding and being clear on expectations.

7. Starting out, Evans named her company Suzanne Evans Coaching, LLC. Today, while her photo is still front and center on the website, Evans envisions a company that is less and less about Suzanne Evans—and more able to survive should something happen to its founder. Her current business model is built on many leadership roles, with a few assistants supporting those roles. The company is divided into divisions, or pods, with managers each running his or her own division.

YOUR NOTES AND REFLECTIONS

_____

_____

_____

_____

_____

_____

_____

_____

_____

_____

_____

_____

_____

_____

_____

_____

_____

_____

_____

_____

_____

_____

Dr. Louay Eldada

Co-founder and Chief Executive Officer,
Quanergy Systems, Inc.

Dr. Eldada is a serial entrepreneur, having founded and sold three businesses to Fortune 100 companies. Quanergy, the leading provider of solid-state LiDAR sensors and smart sensing solutions, is his fourth startup.

Eldada is a technical business leader with a proven record of accomplishment at both small and large companies. With 70 patents, he is a recognized expert in nanotechnology, photonic integrated circuits, and advanced optoelectronics.

Prior to Quanergy, Eldada was CSO of SunEdison, after serving as CTO of HelioVolt, which was acquired by SK Energy. Eldada was earlier CTO of DuPont Photonic Technologies, formed by the acquisition of Telephotonics, where he was founding CTO. His first job was at Honeywell, where he started the Telecom Photonics business and sold it to Corning.

Eldada studied business administration at Harvard, MIT, and Stanford. He holds a Ph.D. in Optical Engineering from Columbia University.

CHAPTER 11

DR. LOUAY ELDADA

When asked to identify a pivotal opportunity or crisis in his life, Louay Eldada
has many experiences from which to choose. Eldada's life has
been anything but dull, and his achievements fall nothing short
of extraordinary.

Eldada's background includes senior-level responsibilities
in research and development; business and technical management; and global strategy at firms that include SunEdison,
DuPont, Corning, and Honeywell. He has sold three startups
to Fortune 100 companies and earned two master degrees plus
a Ph.D. from Columbia University.

Before coming to the United States with $300 and a bag
of used clothes, Eldada lived through most of the civil war in
Lebanon, sometimes running to school in a zigzag to avoid
sniper fire. He often had to negotiate his way out of life or
death situations. For example, Eldada might be stopped at a
checkpoint with his ID showing the wrong religion. In such an
instance, he might have faced death if he didn't know how to
negotiate his way out. "When you grow up with those kinds of
challenges," he says, "everything else becomes easy."

With all this background, when asked to tell about a pivotal life crisis or opportunity, Eldada chose to focus on his experience with Quanergy Systems, Inc.—because the company
represents the one case in which Eldada and his co-founder,
Tianyue Yu, identified a need before the space was hot. The
year was 2012, and the space was autonomous vehicles.

When Eldada and Yu told venture capitalists (VC) they were working on light sensors for vehicles, the response was less than enthusiastic. The VCs gave them a quizzical look, as if the conversation had suddenly turned to science fiction. The VCs just weren't interested. They said, "If the space was hot, we would get more entrepreneurs walking through these doors and talking about it. We are going to pass."

Having done extensive homework before talking to the venture capitalists, Eldada and Yu moved forward without them. The two had inventoried their skills, experience, and strengths, and identified about 30 ideas for the business where they could use those strengths to meet a need—one that wasn't currently being met. The fact that the business could meet a need, of course, was not enough. There had to be customers who were looking for a solution for that same need and were willing to pay a price for it. Eldada says:

You don't start by saying, "Build it, and they will come." You don't say, "I'm just going to do this thing because it is cool." I want to identify how large the need really is, confirm that the customer is passionate about having the need met, and that I have the solution for it. I want to understand why others have not solved this problem. If the need is real, why is no one trying to fill it?

You select from all the needs based on market size, how real the need is, how large it is, the lack of competition, and whether or not you can meet the need with your skill set and experience. Through that systematic selection process, we ended up with LiDAR, a technology that allows us to measure distance by illuminating a target with a laser light to create 3-D mapping.

Given that driver distraction, poor weather, blind spots, and more issues surrounding driver awareness cause 80 percent of car accidents, the team realized they could use LiDAR technology to save lives. Even so, they were careful not to fall in love with the idea too fast—because passion can blind you. They deliberately delayed their passion while focusing on the facts, data, and the voice of the customer. Once they confirmed that all these things were in alignment, they let loose the passion needed to create the solution and the business.

Demonstrating both his belief in the data and his passion for the solution, Eldada was the first investor. Having already sold three startups to Fortune 100 companies, Eldada had the experience and the funding to move forward.

For the first year, the company was in Eldada's home garage. After about a year in the garage, a prototype was ready. During that year, he and his partner continued to collect information and validation through voice of the customers. Then they began to show the demo and the data behind the cost reduction they were able to achieve.

People were skeptical about the concept of cars being able to sense danger and even drive themselves. If such a thing were even possible, it seemed that the level of artificial intelligence needed to make it happen was astounding. Eldada and Yu were claiming they could create this reality in the near future. People thought it impossible that, starting from zero, Quanergy could accomplish such leaps in a few years.

But Quanergy wasn't starting from zero. Eldada had been researching and innovating in this area since working on his Ph.D. at Columbia University 25 years before. The bulk of his Ph.D. work had involved projects with The Defense Advanced Research Projects Agency (DARPA), one of the most innovative organizations in history. Many of the technologies that have changed our lives, including the Internet and satellite, were developed at DARPA and then spread to consumer applications. Eldada says:

This is another case of the core technology being developed at DARPA. The core technology used in our most exciting product is the solid-state LiDAR. LiDAR scans a beam across the environment and gets a million points of the space around you with high accuracy and longer ranges per second, and accomplishes this without any moving parts. This is the part our competitors cannot do. Most of our competitors have mechanical LiDAR.

It's easy to imagine LiDAR like the one on the Google car. It's spinning, so of course it going to see all around, 360 degrees. People can see how that would work. When I say that I can make solid-state LiDAR the size of a credit card, and I can stick it inside a side view mirror or the bumper or behind the grill and it's going to scan the environment without any moving parts on a macro scale and on a micro scale piece, it's a different story. We're not talking about Micro MEMS Mirrors that the naked eye doesn't see but are actually moving—nothing is moving. That blows people's minds.

In addition to knowledge and experience with the technology and the science behind it, Eldada also had relationships in place to outsource manufacturing in cost effective ways. He had been Chief Technology Officer at SunEdison, a projects company that buys and assembles all components of their systems. Quanergy was not starting from zero at all.

Eldada was realistic about how hard it would be to realize the vision behind Quanergy. He knew it would be difficult because he had spent 25 years in the space. Knowing others would fail because the barrier to success was so high, Eldada relied on the team's experience and hard work to make the vision a reality.

One of Quanergy's first big customers was Mercedes, a company with in-house experts who understood the technology on the most fundamental level. They had some experts who had tried themselves and failed to make the technology work. The culture at Mercedes allowed the R & D experts to work with Quanergy with professionalism rather than false pride or fear of losing their jobs. The partnership with Mercedes provided a big boost to the small startup. Quanergy was up and running.

Fast forward to 2016, not all that far from the company's beginnings in 2012. Quanergy Systems, Inc. is the leading provider of LiDAR sensors and smart sensing solutions. These sensors offer significantly lower cost, higher reliability, superior performance, increased capability, smaller size, and lower weight when compared to traditional mechanical sensors. The company's solutions are applicable in numerous sectors, including transportation, mapping, navigation, surveying, security, aeronautics, mining, agriculture, robotics, industrial automation, smart homes, and 3D-aware smart devices for improved safety, efficiency, and performance.

You might say that the space Quanergy occupies is now hot. In fact, according to industry experts, the LiDAR market is expected to exceed $1 billion by 2020 and $3 billion by 2022. In August of 2016, Quanergy announced it had raised $90 million in Series B funding at a valuation well over $1 billion. Sensata Technologies (NYSE:ST), Delphi Automotive (NYSE:DLPH), Samsung Ventures, Motus Ventures and GP Capital participated in the round. This investment brought the company's total funds raised to approximately $150 million.

When interviewed about the new funding, Eldada said:

Innovation in LiDAR technology represents one of the largest opportunities unfolding around the globe, and this infusion of funding will enable us to accelerate development, scale faster, and expand our world-class engineering team. We are grateful for the strong support from so many investors who share our vision of creating intelligent sensing solutions that permeate through multiple industries, significantly improving safety and efficiency. Our investors will be essential partners in our continued growth.

LEADERS BUILD A TEAM WITH
TRUST, LOYALTY, AND COMMUNICATION

Eldada's leadership style was influenced by Larry Bossidy, COO under Jack Welch for 30 years at General Electric. According to Eldada, Bossidy, who was nicknamed Jack's Jackhammer, was actually very fair. Bossidy expected people to prove themselves and earn his respect. He was the type of leader who got to the bottom of things. Once people proved themselves, Bossidy was not a jackhammer to them.

Like Bossidy, Eldada is not soft, but he does inspire loyalty. In fact, some people working with Eldada have been with him through five businesses. When Eldada starts a new venture, he gives certain people a call. Their due diligence is that Eldada is running the show—nothing more is needed.

These people know that, in addition to providing a sound business opportunity and adventure, Eldada cares about his team members as individuals and will take care of them. Eldada realizes that spouses and significant others are part of each individual's big picture. He makes the effort to be aware of what motivates an individual's spouse. Eldada says:

I know them, I know their families, I know their kids' names. I want to see them take good care of their families. And in almost all cases, anyone who has gotten a raise or promotion got it without having to ask for it.

You see the performance and reward that performance without people having to beg for it. This is especially important for technical people who are a bit on the shy side, on the introverted side, who don't like to have to beg for things or recognition. Really, that's mostly what they want. They want to be recognized and rewarded, at least with kind words.

You appreciate what they do, and that's almost enough. Of course, then you reward also financially and with promotions and so on, especially with trust. I don't mi-

cromanage. They appreciate the trust. In return, that
makes them as committed as possible.

With this foundation of trust and loyalty, Eldada leads with boldness, inspiring confidence and even more trust with his team members, including both colleagues and investors. For example, when in the original talks with Mercedes, Eldada predicted things that would happen before these things were confirmed by Mercedes. Knowing that Mercedes liked Quanergy's technology a great deal, Eldada predicted the automobile manufacturer would give Quanergy a free car loaded with half-a-million dollars' worth of equipment, sign a strategic partnership, and do a joint press release.

Of course, this sounded too good to be true—until it all happened. That further built the trust. When it looks like all the parts are in place for something to happen, Eldada takes a risk by saying that thing will happen. This action serves to commit Eldada to make the prediction come true, however hard the process. He creates a vision and then works on achieving that vision.

As prediction and fulfillment happens repeatedly, Eldada and Quanergy gain more and more credibility. Each time Eldada makes a promise and delivers on it, the trust and credibility increases. For his part, Eldada has to make the predictions come true.

LEADERS CREATE CULTURE

For the first year, Quanergy consisted of Eldada and his co-founder, Yu, whom Eldada describes as brilliant. Yu is an innovative technical leader with corporations and startups. In addition to impressive technical expertise, she has analytical and problem-solving skills that help overcome complex problems at the intersection of multiple disciplines. Eldada is proud that his co-founder is a woman, believing that if everyone hired the most capable person regardless of anything else, the world would have a 50-50 split of men and women in all positions.

After the first year, Eldada began to build his executive team—slowly. Eldada does not hire people he does not know and he does not rush to put them in their ultimate positions. As an experienced founder, he has learned to avoid hiring people simply because they have the talent and titles. He says, "If someone doesn't buy into the vision and want to be part of it regardless of title, I don't want them here." In fact, only recently did he promote the final two members of his executive team to vice presidents. Eldada had held them at a director level for 18 months until they proved themselves. Then he surprised them with a promotion they didn't have to ask for.

Eldada points to companies that like to introduce their products with shock and awe. These companies hire people, offering big salaries and big titles, essentially buying them for the company. Eldada says, "If I was able to buy someone, someone else might be able to pay a higher price and get them. That's not the kind of talent I want."

Once a week, Eldada holds an alignment meeting with Quanergy's executive team. Once a month, he holds a town hall meeting for all the employees, encouraging them to ask the most difficult or embarrassing questions. If someone believes there is something he or she cannot say, Eldada wants to hear it. This doesn't mean he answers everything, but he answers what he can. If leaking a deal that is in process might kill the deal, Eldada will explain that something is going on that he can't talk about. He won't pretend nothing is going on.

Eldada works to create a culture of transparency and candid feedback. He says:

I'm not looking for people to flatter me. Actually, I get terrified when people flatter me because I stay away from "yes" people. They're not helping me. They're not helping themselves. I don't trust them. They make me nauseous.

When it comes to hiring, Eldada hires for attitude as much as aptitude. He says, "It's 50-50. If you give someone an A on aptitude but give them an F on attitude, that's a C. I don't want to hire a C."

Given that culture is so important, the company has a list of top 10 core values that everyone knows. If you walk around the offices at Quanergy, you'll likely see the list sitting on everyone's desk.

In weekly one-on-one meetings with his directors, Eldada ensures that the directors are aligned on the cultural aspects of the company. He also gives candid feedback and helps his team members to grow, both inside the company and in external learning experiences.

GOOD LEADERS LEARN FROM OTHER GOOD LEADERS

Eldada grew up with humble beginnings in Lebanon. After avoiding snipers on his way to and from school, Eldada studied all night by candlelight. Hard work brought him top scores in his class. Eldada was motivated to work hard by an opportunity he credits to the late Rafic Hariri.

Hariri was a successful Lebanese businessman and former Prime Minister of Lebanon. Hariri is credited with reconstructing the capital Beirut after the civil war. According to Eldada, Hariri was also a person who rewarded talent when he saw it, even before he served as prime minister. Hariri took care of people without expecting anything in return. From Hariri, Eldada learned that if you pick the right people and take care of them, they will give back without you having to ask for it.

Eldada gives Hariri credit for his education and the belief that if he did all that he could, he would succeed, even with his humble beginnings. Eldada says:

> *My experience is the opposite of growing up in an afflu-ent family where everything is given to you, and you don't have to try hard. Between the civil war experience, and having someone as an angel, I made it. Mr. Rafic*

Hariri was an angel on earth and an angel in heaven now. He changed my life. I'm still in touch with his family.

Another significant influence on Eldada's life was Larry Bossidy, whom Eldada worked under at General Electric for six years. Bossidy, with Ram Charan, is author of *Execution: The Discipline of Getting Things Done.*

In Bossidy, Eldada sees a straight shooter who gives candid feedback—not to be nasty, but to be honest. Bossidy doesn't have room for mediocrity. He is careful to hire capable people and trust them by getting out of their way. When a person is not capable, Bossidy lets them go quickly because accepting mediocrity leads to a mediocre company.

Eldada also admires and is inspired by another leader who is featured in this book, Ossama Hassanein. Dr. Hassanein exemplifies a person who helps and appreciates capable people. Eldada says, "By helping others, you also lift yourself because you have high caliber people surrounding you."

Eldada incorporates the lessons from mentors into his leadership—and he keeps learning. CXO forums and other venues help Eldada stay in touch with great minds outside of Quanergy. He participates in such forums, not so much to talk as to listen. Eldada is forever learning, believing he will never be arrogant, because the more he learns, the more he realizes how little he knows, the more he realizes things can always be improved. He says, "I reach out to all kinds of cultures that have different wisdoms. You learn from looking and listening on a global level. There's just lots of wisdom that you can learn from both Western and Eastern cultures."

ADVICE TO EMERGING LEADERS

Asked to share advice with emerging entrepreneurs and leaders, Eldada gives three quick responses:

1. HIRE PEOPLE WHO ARE SMARTER THAN YOU ARE
    In Eldada's experience, the people who want to be
    the smartest ones in the room are the ones who fail.
    The ones who surround themselves with capable
    people and nurture their talents are the ones who
    succeed.

2. HELP OTHERS TO OWN THE
    IDEAS THEY WORK TO EXECUTE
    Even when a leader finds himself or herself more
    knowledgeable than others, the leader does well to
    sit back, relax, and let others own the process. If the
    leader has an idea, it's best to "drop heads" and help
    others come up with the idea. Individuals aren't mo-
    tivated and energized to run with the leader's ideas.
    When the ideas come from themselves, they own
    them and the leader can walk away and move to
    other things.

3. AVOID TAKING CREDIT
    Good leaders don't take credit. They support and
    appreciate others by giving them the credit and
    walking away. When the leader does this, the team
    ends up supporting and lifting the leader. The best
    way to be selfish is to be selfless.

As Quanergy continues to seize the global opportunity that
LiDAR affords, Louay Eldada will continue to be an exceptional leader. He will continue to surround himself with capable people, nurturing their talent and recognizing their accomplishments. The foundation of trust and loyalty, as well as a
culture aligned with values, is already there. We can count on
Eldada to continue building on that foundation—and changing
our world with Quanergy innovation.

SUMMARY

1. Louay Eldada is CEO & Co-founder, Quanergy Systems. His background includes senior-level responsibilities in research and development; business and technical management; and global strategy at firms that include SunEdison, DuPont, Corning, and Honeywell. He has sold three startups to Fortune 100 companies and earned two master degrees plus a Ph.D. from Columbia University.

2. When Eldada and his co-founder, Tianyue Yu, pitched the idea of light sensors for vehicles to venture capitalists in 2012, investors were far from enthusiastic. They were skeptical about the concept of cars being able to sense danger and even drive themselves. It seemed that the level of artificial intelligence needed to make such a thing happen would be astounding. Eldada and Yu were claiming they could create this reality in the near future.

3. The two founders forged ahead without the venture capitalists. Eldada had been researching and innovating in this area since working on his Ph.D. at Columbia University 25 years before, so the company was not starting from zero. They built the first prototype in Eldada's garage.

4. Today, Quanergy Systems, Inc. is the leading provider of LiDAR sensors and smart sensing solutions. These sensors offer significantly lower cost, higher reliability, superior performance, increased capability, smaller size, and lower weight when compared to traditional mechanical sensors. The company's solutions are applicable in numerous sectors, improving safety, efficiency, and performance. In August of 2016, Quanergy announced it had raised $90 million in Series B funding at a valuation well over $1 billion.

5. Growing up in humble beginnings in Lebanon, Eldada lived through most of the civil war before moving to the United States. He credits the late Rafic Hariri, a successful Lebanese businessman and former Prime Minister of

Lebanon, with providing him with an important opportunity and life lesson in his youth. From Hariri, Eldada learned that if you pick the right people and take care of them, they will give back without you having to ask for it.

6. When it came to hiring an executive team, Eldada was slow and careful. He believes that if he can "buy" talent, someone else can "buy" that talent away. He says, "If someone doesn't buy into the vision and want to be part of it regardless of title, I don't want them here." He doesn't rush to give people fancy titles, but eventually surprises them with promotions once they have proven themselves.

7. Eldada works to create a culture of transparency and candid feedback, avoiding "yes" people because he believes such people are neither helpful nor trustworthy. Once a week, Eldada holds an alignment meeting with Quanergy's executive team. Once a month, he holds a town hall meeting for all the employees, encouraging them to ask the most difficult or embarrassing questions.

8. Eldada believes in building trust by knowing people's families and by rewarding performance without being asked to do so. This is especially important for technical people who are a bit on the shy side and don't like to have to beg for recognition. Appreciating what people do is almost enough, but you also reward them financially and with promotions.

9. Eldada incorporates the lessons from mentors into his leadership—and he keeps learning. He participates in CXO forums and other venues to stay in touch with great minds outside of Quanergy. He participates in such forums, not so much to talk as to listen. Eldada is forever learning, believing he will never be arrogant, because the more he learns, the more he realizes how little he knows, the more he realizes things can always be improved.

Your Notes and Reflections

_____

_____

_____

_____

_____

_____

_____

_____

_____

_____

_____

_____

_____

_____

_____

VINCE PIZZICA
Senior Executive Vice President,
Technicolor Corporation

Vince Pizzica is a leading executive in the ICT and media industries with specialized experience in strategic turnarounds. He has strong skills in translating strategy into operational plans and actions.

On September 1, 2008, Vince Pizzica began his job at Thomson SA, a historic and iconic French company with global business. On September 15, the Lehman Brothers meltdown occurred and a large investor pulled out. Pizzica and CEO, Frederick Rose, navigated the French bankruptcy process and led the company to rebranding as Technicolor and solid footing.

Prior to joining Technicolor, he oversaw Technology, Strategy & Marketing at Alcatel-Lucent for the EMEA and APAC regions.

Over a 20-plus year career in the telecoms industry, Pizzica's responsibilities have included CTO for the APAC region at Alcatel-Lucent, General Manager of the Trusted Networks activity at Siemens in Australia, and various roles in operations and technology at Telstra.

Australian by birth, Pizzica holds a Bachelor in Engineering degree from the Institute of Engineers and a Master in Science degree in Telecommunications and Information Systems from the University of Essex in the United Kingdom.

CHAPTER 12

VINCE PIZZICA

On September 1, 2008, Vince Pizzica began his job at Thomson SA, a historic and iconic French company with global business. Unfortunately, the company was in bad shape.

Together, Pizzica and Frederic Rose (CEO of Technicolor, the new brand for Thomson) had recently decided to leave their positions at Alcatel-Lucent and look for a leadership challenge, one at which they could prove themselves. The two came on board at Thomson with the encouragement of a large investor, Silver Lake, which had a $500 million convertible note coming due on September 16. When Pizzica and Rose joined on September 1, Silver Lake was committed to helping Thomson turn around. On September 15, as the Lehman Brothers meltdown occurred, Silver Lake decided to get their money and pull out.

Pizzica describes the situation:

Here we were, with a dramatically weakened balance sheet, because we had just paid half a billion dollars to Silver Lake. The world was melting down all around us, and the people who had encouraged us to come on board to try to help turn the company around had just left. It was a cyclone of change, and there were many things wrong with the company.

Today, rebranded as Technicolor, the company is on solid footing once again. But in late 2008, Pizzica and Rose were facing years of sorting things out and getting the organization on a successful track. It took two years to guide the company through the French bankruptcy process, stabilize operations to generate positive cash flows consistently, and rebuild the balance sheet to the point at which they could start making acquisitions.

One segment of the problem at the company involved the existing management. Many of the managers couldn't see the problems that had been created over many years, so they couldn't easily be a part of the solution. Others saw the problems, but didn't necessarily have the tools or understanding needed to get out of the mess. A major management shakeup was needed.

Another segment of the problem involved culture and focus. Although the company had a strong global footprint, it was decidedly French in its DNA, headquartered in Paris, with a strong French component in the management team. Despite this, the revenue profile of the business was predominantly North American. The company needed a dramatic cultural shift to better understand its markets, as well as a renewed focus on making sure the bank balance increased each month.

Yet another portion of the problem involved the company's portfolio of businesses. Having made 40-50 acquisitions over a five-year period, Thomson was a much more diverse company than the telecom companies in which Pizzica had worked. Pizzica describes it this way:

When you are sitting there with this new hand of cards you've been dealt, you're trying to understand, "Okay, what do I keep and what don't I keep?" You've really got to take a step back and look at each of these businesses, try and understand what they're doing, and try to understand what their prospects for the future are. You need to assess the underlying profitability of the markets they are in, their competitive position, so on and so on. We did most of that analysis over the first three months and then made choices about what we thought was the right portfolio of businesses to go forward.

It was a lot of turmoil in the first three to six months, and we were very much in a cyclone. We were putting in long days, trying to sustain the motivation of our teams and trying to keep the edges from getting frazzled, because people's feelings were a bit hurt over all the rapid changes.

During this initial phase, Rose was CEO and Pizzica was Senior Executive Vice President (SEVP). Very early on, they began to realize that some of the CFO's decision-making was not on the same wavelength as theirs, and they felt the need to bring in a new member to the inner team to replace him.

With that change, these top three executives were all new to the company. They had to get connected to the current company while making and implementing decisions about the future in a truncated timeframe.

Nothing illegal had been going on, but the new executive team kept uncovering a need to reset the way the company was managing itself financially. That involved communicating in a frank manner to roughly 50 different creditors and eventually deciding to take the company through the French bankruptcy process (known as sauvegarde) so that they could properly reset its capital structure.

Fortunately, there was an agreement among the new three top executives, and they held all the stakeholders together. Together, they were able to focus on saving the company.

GOOD COMMUNICATION
BEGINS WITH LISTENING—AND THEN ACTING

As the executive management team worked to turn the company around, they knew they needed to communicate, connect, and learn from the people who made up this complex international company. There were many different languages, both literal and metaphorical, in which to communicate.

The CEO and new members of the management team invested time in visiting sites and answering questions from employees, especially in the earliest months, as they progressed toward making decisions about the future. Pizzica especially remembers visiting sites in Germany and the United States. He focused on the technology, research, and marketing teams, seeking to learn what they were doing as well as their perspectives regarding opportunities and challenges.

As the time for implementing their changes came, the team held a combination of town halls and video interview sessions across the various key sites of Thomson. They anticipated questions and made sure those were addressed. They also sent e-mails from the CEO to all employees every two to three months, providing updates to further help employees feel informed and connected to the changes.

During a time of crisis, according to Pizzica, leaders must communicate even more than normal. Employees need a level of transparency from the leadership team so they can continue to feel loyal and connected to a purpose or mission. Of course, employees also need to have a sense of stability to help alleviate their anxieties about their livelihood.

In addition to communicating with employees, the new Thomson management team also had to communicate with other stakeholders, particularly with the investor community. The previous management had unsettled confidence in the company through many missed targets and confusing messages. Investors were struggling to believe in what the company said anymore, so the new leaders needed to invest time and energy to rebuild trust. This was ultimately achieved through an initial town hall session involving a large cross section of investor stakeholders at the start of the sauvegarde process, followed by more detailed one-on-one meetings over the months ahead.

Employees and investors weren't the only stakeholders who had grown wary of the company. Customers were concerned and anxious about the challenges as well. It was essential to re-engage customer confidence in long-term certainty of the company as a partner. Pizzica says:

> *We certainly uncovered crazy cultural things. At the time, the parent company was still called Thomson, and for whatever reason, management had decided that every business in the company was going to be rebranded as Thomson–even storied brands like Technicolor, Grass Valley, and the boutique visual effects company known as Moving Picture Company. They were going to just change the name of everything and put everyone into the same brand without really understanding what was going on inside those businesses. On the first day that we turned up at Technicolor in Los Angeles, the sign on the building said Technicolor by Thomson, yet 'Thomson' was actually in bigger font than Technicolor on the sign. We said to each other, "Okay, there's a problem here."*
>
> *When we talked to customers, we learned they were considerably anxious about the branding as well. Customers had been doing business with Technicolor for nearly a hundred years. Suddenly, the name was changing. Customers needed to maintain confidence in the company they were doing business with, but they had no day-to-day exposure to Thomson.*
>
> *We developed a 'house of brands' strategy. We quickly discarded the plans to name everything Thomson. We spoke to the people at each brand and said, "Hey, we treasure the way you guys work as a team; we understand that you have a system of customers and partners. While you work under that broader company called Thomson, we want you to keep your identity." That built trust with them, and released some of the pressure on change, because those weren't the things to change.*

There were plenty of other things to change, but this wasn't one of them.

EFFECTIVE LEADERS ARE TEACHERS WHO ARE ALWAYS LEARNING

The task at Thomson reinforced lessons Pizzica had learned earlier in his career, but also provided some new leadership lessons as well.

Having always embraced diversity in management teams, Pizzica found his commitment to diversity challenged, primarily because Pizzica found the new CFO a difficult person to form a personal relationship with. Prior to his position at Thomson, Pizzica had always been in teams where members found ways to also be good friends away from work. This wasn't the case in this new environment, yet Pizzica and the CFO worked well together on the bigger mission, the broader objectives. He understood and respected that the CEO needed both inputs, and that he and the CFO didn't have to agree, and in fact were often going to be in conflict. In fact, Pizzica believes the focus on the broader objectives and the importance of the team rather than the individual dynamic between him and the CFO was, on reflection, an aspect of their success.

In his own development as a leader, Pizzica has been fortunate to have good mentors both internal and external to the companies where he worked. In his 20s, as part of a development program, Pizzica met a psychologist who explained Myers-Briggs to him. With his interest sparked, Pizzica spent time with psychologists, learning about personality types and how those personality types work in teams. He quickly developed skill in identifying how differing approaches to conceptualizing, processing, and making decisions benefits a team in problem solving. From that time on, Pizzica actively sought to build diverse teams.

At 31, as the youngest technology executive at Telstra at that time, Pizzica sought a lot of input on what he needed to do and how to do it. He actively sought out external mentors, many of whom were CEOs of companies in the industry or even adjacent companies, to get their perspectives on commercial issues or handling management styles.

Pizzica mentions Frank Blount, who was CEO during Pizzica's rise at Telstra, as an individual whose thinking and strategic approach to organizations he admires. Pizzica watched as Blount led Telstra through a cultural and strategic transition so it could eventually move from being a government agency to a public company. Rather than merely envision Telstra as he wanted it to be, Blount identified the key things that would be important for a successful transition. He was also smart enough to identify the strengths in the current culture and to build on those. The whole process took time and patience. Pizzica says:

> *I remember being in a meeting where Blount talked about how the journey we were on at Telstra was a seven-year journey. At the time, I heard this, but I didn't understand it. As I went through our major change at Thomson, I finally understood what Blount was talking about.*

> *I respect the fact that Blount put in place the framework for change by looking at culture, values, vision, and something he called a Balance of Consequences Framework. This, basically, was saying, "We've taught people to do the wrong thing, because as a company, we've usually rewarded them when they've acted with the wrong behaviors whilst we should have been telling them that they were wrong. When people have done the right things, we haven't consistently given them the appropriate rewards."*

> *Blount forced his leadership team to think about the behaviors they wanted, how they responded to those behaviors, and how they responded when people did the wrong behaviors. He made us all think that way about our teams at Telstra. A good example of the more gen-*

eral principle Blount had is, "As a leader, you need to be a teacher and a communicator."

Pizzica is aware that there are always opportunities to teach. People make mistakes, and a leader needs to help people learn from the mistakes rather than feel bad about them. In addition to teaching, Pizzica places a priority on continually learning. Recently, he has begun to look again for external mentors, with a focus on the industry level in the San Francisco Bay Area. Pizzica is developing his understanding of venture investing as an important tool for the ways in which innovation is changing, and how to create value from innovation.

LEADING CHANGE REQUIRES COURAGE AND PERSEVERANCE

At Thomson, the new management team members knew they needed to change the style of decision-making. To survive the tight constraints they had on cash flow, the company had to move into a more command/control style to meet their new debt covenants in sauvegarde. The team knew such changes would have cultural consequences, but they also knew they had no choice.

It was difficult to help front-line managers understand that the changes weren't so much about distrusting people who were in decision-making positions as they were about the need to hit cash targets every month. The management team told employees, "For the next little while, you've got to trust us; the decision making has to come from the center."

Obviously, there was a period of fear when the company let go of some of the middle levels of management. Naturally, people had moments of wondering who was next to go. On top of that, everyone knew there were plans to sell or close some businesses to simplify the portfolio of the company. The team had to go public with this strategy and to keep walking people through the broader mission that was at hand. Pizzica says:

You can't deny the fact that at some point tough deci-
sions have to be made. Once those decisions are made,
it's critical to get out there and communicate. It's inevi-
table that these tough decisions may end up hurting
some people and their feelings, so you need to expect
that and try to treat everyone with respect.

At Thomson, it took more than a year for the structural changes to be made. Throughout that time, the new management
team kept working through the cultural impacts. They kept
asking what values they had, what values they wanted people
to treasure, and how to create a desirable association with the
brand. They worked on rebranding the company because these
leaders knew they had an opportunity for people to come out
of the restructuring phase with loyalty to a new brand, given
all of the damage and hurt that the various stakeholders had
experienced under the Thomson brand. A new brand could become both the symbol of change at the company and the rally-
ing force behind a return to growth.

Throughout 2009, the team listened to employees, heard
what people thought was important, and what values they
wanted to see the company reflect. They talked to customers
about what they treasured about the company and how those
elements affected the relationship.

As the company went through bankruptcy, some of the
customers who had worked with the company for many years,
including Warner Brothers and Disney, went out of their way
to renew contracts, even though they didn't need to do so at
that time. This sent the signal that these customers believed in
the company. The leaders used this positive market signal as a
message to their own employees, saying, "Hey, you can believe in our company because our customers believe in us."
Early in 2010, they successfully relaunched the brand as
Technicolor.

Advice for Emerging Leaders

When asked to give advice to leaders who seek to make a big change, Pizzica distills his recommendations down to a few simple things:

1. ### Create a Plan and Structure
   Many leaders bounce around on change without a rough idea of where they are going. Leaders at high levels are trying to solve problems, and they need to have an idea of where they want to go. Pizzica recommends creating some sort of plan, structure, or sequence to work through. It's okay to challenge the plan, but it's ineffective to try to move forward without one.

2. ### Stay honest and keep
   #### lines of communication open
   When a leader gives people as much information as he or she can, that leader builds trust, which is essential. Working with people at a human level makes them more likely to get on board with tougher decisions that need to happen for successful change. The goal is to have everyone go on the same mission, with people feeling like they are part of the change, not victims of it.

3. ### Cultivate patience
   Change takes time, especially at the cultural level. Pizzica says, "Someone once said to me that I'm a very calm leader, that when things go wrong, I don't overreact. I think I would put that to being more patient. I expect that things are going to go wrong sometimes. I'm patient with the process and accept that things don't always go right the first time."

   Pizzica recommends stepping back and making sure you are fighting the right fight. He cautions leaders not to get confused between tactics and strategy because he often sees managers get too wedded to tactics or lose sight on bigger goals when pursuing their short-term objectives. When a leader steps back and takes a good look at what is going on, that leader has a better chance of knowing what he or she should be doing and what is the more important priority.

Pizzica is an example of a leader who habitually steps back, listens, and prioritizes before acting. His Technicolor story demonstrates how a leadership team assessed culture, identified core values, and introduced change with respect, authentic communication, and patience.

Summary

1. When Vince Pizzica and Frederick Rose joined Thomson
    SA on September 1, 2008, the large investor, Silver Lake,
    was committed to helping the struggling company turn
    around. On September 15, as the Lehman Brothers melt-
    down occurred, Silver Lake decided to get their money
    and pull out.

2. Today, rebranded as Technicolor, the company is on solid
    footing once again. But in late 2008, Pizzica and Rose
    faced years of sorting things out and getting the organiza-
    tion on a successful track. Getting back on track included
    going through the French bankruptcy process, stabilizing
    operations to generate consistently positive cash flows,
    and rebuilding the balance sheet to the point at which they
    could start making acquisitions.

3. The first three to six months held its share of turmoil, as
    the new leaders analyzed each of the many businesses that
    made up the company, and sought to understand their pro-
    spects for the future. At the same time, they were trying to
    sustain the motivation of their teams.

4. As the executive management team, including a new
    CFO, worked to turn the company around, they knew they
    needed to communicate, connect, and learn from the peo-
    ple who made up this complex international company.
    Employees needed a level of transparency from the lead-
    ership team so they could continue to feel loyal and con-
    nected to a purpose. Employees also needed to have a
    sense of stability to help alleviate their anxieties about
    their livelihood. As the time for implementing their
    change came, the leadership team held a combination of
    town halls and video interview sessions across the various
    key sites of Thomson.

5. It took more than a year for the structural changes to be
    made. Throughout that time, the executive team kept
    working through the cultural impacts and listening to em-

ployees. They kept asking what values they had, what values they wanted people to treasure, and how to create a desirable association with the brand. The leaders saw re-branding as an opportunity for people to come out of the restructuring phase with loyalty to a new brand, given all of the hurt the various stakeholders had experienced under the Thomson brand.

6. Customers were concerned about a blanket branding change that Thomson had initiated before the new leaders came on board. In response, the executive team developed a 'house of brands' strategy, in which each brand retained its own identity under the broader company called Thomson. That built trust and released some of the pressure on change.

7. In his own development as a leader, Pizzica has appreciated good mentors both inside and external to the companies where he worked, and he believes in continually learning. He admires Frank Blount, who was CEO during Pizzica's tenure as a rising leader at Telstra. Pizzica watched as Blount led Telstra through a cultural and strategic transition so it could eventually move from being a government agency to a public company. From Blount, Pizzica learned, among other things, that leaders need to be teachers and communicators.

8. When asked to give advice to leaders who seek to make a big change, Pizzica distills his recommendations down to a few critical things: Create a plan and structure; stay honest and keep lines of communication open; and cultivate patience.

Your Notes and Reflections

_____

_____

_____

_____

_____

_____

_____

_____

_____

_____

_____

_____

_____

_____

_____

Dr. Rosina L. Racioppi
President and Chief Executive Officer,
WOMEN Unlimited, Inc.

As President and CEO of WOMEN Unlimited, Inc., Dr. Rosina Racioppi spearheads her organization's initiatives to help Fortune 1000 companies cultivate the talent needed for ongoing growth and profitability. Under her leadership, WOMEN Unlimited, Inc. successfully partners with organizations across a wide range of industries to develop their high-potential women and build a pipeline of diverse and talented leaders.

Prior to joining WOMEN Unlimited, Inc., Racioppi held executive management positions in human resources at Degussa Corporation, Nextran (a division of Baxter Corporation), and Beechwood Data Systems. She has over 25 years' experience in organization planning and development; compensation and benefits; training and development; safety; quality management; staffing, and employee relations.

Racioppi holds a BA in Criminal Justice from Michigan State University and an M.Ed. from the Univerity of Pennsylvania. She earned her doctorate in education from the University of Pennsylvania. Her dissertation, "Women's Mentoring Wisdom," focuses on how women use and fail to use mentoring at the all-important mid-career level.

CHAPTER 13

DR. ROSINA L. RACIOPPI

Rosina Racioppi was interested in business strategy and profitability as far back as she can remember. Going through files at one of her high school jobs, Racioppi noticed that the attorney she worked for had clients with outstanding balances. Realizing she couldn't receive a paycheck if the firm wasn't profitable, Racioppi took it upon herself to send out letters to clients in arrears.

Years later, as a young professional in human resources (HR) in manufacturing, Racioppi continued to understand the importance of business strategy and profitability. She made a point to connect with the people in operations. Wanting to understand how operations worked and how HR could support the P&L side of the business, Racioppi invited herself to strategy meetings. Racioppi learned that she loved business. As a neutral party, she could see things that others, too deep in the weeds, couldn't see. Racioppi became an advisor to the operational team.

By the time Racioppi joined WOMEN Unlimited, Inc. nearly 20 years ago, she was as interested in the business side of the firm as she was in its mission. She was also well prepared to support Jean Otte, who founded the company in 1994. Racioppi worked for a number of years as a business development leader within the North region before transitioning to President and CEO during the difficult economic years of 2007 and 2008.

WOMEN Unlimited is a world-renowned organization, focusing on developing women leaders in major corporations.

Because of its ability to pinpoint, develop, and retain diverse high-potential leadership talent, WOMEN Unlimited is the go-to development partner for over 160 leading organizations.

The organization works in partnership with Fortune 1000 corporations to provide a three-pronged approach to developing women. The three prongs are mentoring, education, and networking. This comprehensive approach helps women to develop the skills and mindset shifts they need to become the next generation of top executives. Programs focus on emerging women leaders, those transitioning from managing to leadership, and senior executives. With a solid history of success, the company can boast that 96 percent of their corporate partners come back to them repeatedly to select and develop their high-potential women.

At the time Racioppi took over as President and CEO, WOMEN Unlimited was roughly 15 years old. The company was successful and growing. Because Jean Otte, Nina Dougar (CFO and partial owner), and Racioppi were committed to a positive transition, they began planning for the transition several years before the actual transition occurred. Good leadership requires creating a plan for a sustainable future for the organization.

Good Leadership
Involves Clarity and Conversation

As her own first step in the transition, Racioppi took a step back and performed an assessment of what was working and where she felt tension in the business. She had noticed that the firm's messaging was not resonating as strongly in conversations with some new companies. She wanted to know why and what shifts were needed for the company to move forward productively.

To get an objective perspective, WOMEN Unlimited hired a firm to do a deep market assessment. The assessment —including conversations with the WOMEN Unlimited team members, corporate partners, and companies that had chosen not to become partners—allowed the firm to clarify its direction to ensure a sustainable future: The ideal corporate partner for WOMEN Unlimited is an organization that desires to build a diverse talent pipeline as a business strategy, not an activity.

This fresh clarity helped the firm to give more direction to the individuals responsible to build relationships with target organizations. Racioppi says:

We are a small organization with limited resources, occupying a space where we get many opportunities, but not all the opportunities are worthy of our attention. We need to make certain we focus on those activities that foster the growth we are targeting. As a first step, we created a framework to assess opportunities that allowed us to manage the business productively.

Although everyone in the firm knew Racioppi, change in leadership is always challenging. While Racioppi's leadership was the next logical chapter in the organization, her vision was not exactly the same as the founder's.

Many of the firm's employees were women who had been part of the organization since its inception. Racioppi wanted to maintain the strong talent within the organization and keep team members focused on growing the story of WOMEN Unlimited beyond where it started.

The leadership team expanded the board and also hired a coach to work with them around how they were evolving as an organization, how the roles were changing, and how they needed to support one another. This process, involving open, transparent conversations, aligns with what WOMEN Unlimited teaches clients in their programs. To be effective in business, it's important to create a team that can have honest dialogue to address issues before they become major challenges or obstacles.

The conversations created a rhythm of open dialogue and shared perspective. This was especially important to Racioppi because she knows that no leader can possibly know and see everything. As she stepped into her new role, Racioppi needed to create pathways of communication within the team so that she could understand what was happening and assess alignment within the organization. She had to ensure the team members were communicating and sharing a common vision as the organization evolved.

At the same time WOMEN Unlimited was transitioning to a new president and CEO, the economy was facing severe challenges. Racioppi prefers to think of this as a shift in business climate rather than a crisis. As a businessperson, she seeks to be cognizant of, and plan for, continual challenges in business climate. Talk of crisis tends to lead people into panic rather than into positive directions.

GOOD LEADERSHIP INVOLVES
SUSTAINABLE STRATEGIES AND RELATIONSHIPS

From its inception, WOMEN Unlimited has intentionally kept a strong internal reserve to help manage through difficult times. The leaders made specific strategic decisions about how to manage if the economy would negatively affect programs. The company faced the economic downturn with a goal of maintaining presence even if the programs were affected. They were committed to maintaining relationships with corporate partners and staff. And they didn't want anyone to lose her job. In the face of the economic downturn in 2007 and 2008, the leadership team chose to cut their own compensation so that no one else had to be negatively affected.

Speaking of the firm's perspective on clients, Racioppi says:

We use the term, corporate partner, as more than a label. This term defines the relationship. While WOMEN Unlimited is essentially a vendor, we treat relationships with clients as partnerships. We want to know what's going on in our partner companies. Each company is slightly different, and we want to understand how we fit into their strategies so we can help them be successful. If they are successful, we are successful.

Many of their partners were challenged during the financial crisis, without budgets to participate in WOMEN Unlimited programs. These partners still needed to maintain certain tools to retain diverse talent. WOMEN Unlimited worked with their partners to create workable strategies. Sometimes they delayed invoicing or simply kept the partner engaged in low cost ways. This allowed partners to stay involved with WOMEN Unlimited and not lose ground until the budgets came back around.

During this time, Racioppi reminded her team that WOMEN Unlimited's success depended upon the success of their corporate partners, using the image of the ebb and flow of the tide. When the tide is ebbing, it's hard to see how internal processes will support the success the company could expect on the backend of the financial crisis. Racioppi told her team:

Let's use this time wisely. While we can, let's shore up any cracks and make sure we are ready for the tide when it rises. Let's make sure we don't have leaks throughout the organization. Let's work to ensure we will have a stronger organization coming out of the downturn.

This perspective helped team members have a more positive experience. The organization took a hit, and it took time for partner companies to come around. Yet, because WOMEN Unlimited worked with the realities of their clients, they maintained all of their corporate partners. The partners just spent less during those years of crisis.

GOOD LEADERSHIP CREATES CLARITY AROUND TIME, ATTENTION, AND DEPTH

An effective CEO is mindful of her presence as the face of the organization. She is also intentional about how she spends her time and how she prepares others to step into growth roles. Racioppi thought a lot about these things as she planned her transition to the company's top leadership role.

She explains the process like this, "It's really knowing thyself and creating the guardrails for where your attention needs to be. This is not something that happens overnight."

Focused attention is not easy, and letting go of roles you love can be a challenge. Racioppi loved business development but knew she needed to help other people grow to perform that part of the business. She needed to be clear with the organization and her team about what she, as CEO, needed to do. Racioppi asked her board to hold her accountable to focus on critical tasks, not flip back to ones that are comfortable.

Racioppi believes that one of the roles of an organization's top leader is to ensure the firm has the credentials and validation to do what it does. She was aware that Otte had founded WOMEN Unlimited with experience as a senior executive at National Car Rental.

Racioppi's experience certainly qualified her to lead WOMEN Unlimited. Prior to joining the firm, she held executive management positions in human resources at Degussa Corporation, Nextran (a division of Baxter Corporation), and Beechwood Data Systems. In addition to her role in business development and senior leadership position at WOMEN Unlimited, Racioppi had extensive experience in organization planning and development; compensation and benefits; training and development, safety; quality management; staffing; and employee relations. She held a Bachelor's Degree in Criminal Justice from Michigan State University.

To maintain the organization's depth and credentials, Racioppi decided to go back to school to earn her doctorate in education from the University of Pennsylvania. Her dissertation, "Women's Mentoring Wisdom," focuses on how women use and fail to use mentoring at the all-important mid-career level.

Racioppi decided to earn her doctorate, with support from her business partners, as a strategic initiative. She stepped up to the challenge and collaborated with the other leaders to manage the business while she completed this degree. The result yielded more than credentials that validate the company's mission. The doctorate program, which focuses on work-based learning, gave Racioppi rich insight to strengthen what the organization does. It was an investment on all sides to strengthen the foundation of WOMEN Unlimited.

Racioppi's credentials and experience are only one example of the depth that WOMEN Unlimited provides partner corporations. Other firms, of course, provide development programs for women. Because of the context and structure of WOMEN Unlimited programs, however, this company gets a unique sense of what women are currently facing. While other organizations may be conducting surveys, WOMAN Unlimited managers and facilitators are holding frank conversations with women and mentors in extended programs.

These conversations reveal patterns, challenges, and concerns, as well as strategies women are employing in today's marketplace. Because of the breadth and depth of these conversations, WOMEN Unlimited can provide insights without breaking confidences or trust, a sacred commitment to partners.

WOMEN Unlimited aggregates information to help partners understand the challenges women currently face at the emerging, mid-career, and senior level. This information is important because it comes objectively from outside any partner organization. A real-time snapshot can provide a competitive edge in recruiting and retaining diverse talent.

With conversations surrounding this information, WOMEN Unlimited reaches beyond the women enrolled in their programs. The conversations allow for a genuine partnership with managers and mentors—including the men in the organization. In this way, WOMEN Unlimited is in a unique position to support an organization's desire to have women advancing in the organization.

Women and men experience things differently. Men who lead women experience this as a challenge. Male leaders don't necessarily understand what they need to do to support women properly. This might mean that women don't receive the feedback or advice they need to develop. This lack doesn't occur because men don't want women to be successful, but because they don't understand how women are experiencing the organization.

WOMEN Unlimited recognizes that the value they provide to male leaders is a unique opportunity to their partners. At no cost, a woman participant can select a male leader to participate as a mentor. The only cost is time. WOMEN Unlimited supports the mentors so that they are not working in a vacuum. The mentors gain valuable insight that helps their own careers. In fact, corporate partners are increasingly choosing this mentoring opportunity as part of their development of high-potential male leaders.

ADVICE FOR EMERGING LEADERS

When asked what advice she would give to young women just starting a career, Racioppi makes the following four suggestions:

1. DEVELOP THE HABIT OF CURIOSITY
   According to Racioppi, it's easy to graduate from college thinking you are "all that and a bag of chips." Knowing you are smart and that you've completed a rigorous school program can lead to a type of blind arrogance.

   Young women need to understand that while they may be smart, they don't know everything. We all have limited knowledge and experience. A habit of curiosity is an asset. Rather than judge someone else as wrong, seek to understand why that person has a different perspective. Try to figure out what you are missing.

2. DON'T DO IT ALONE

   This piece of advice is repeated often in WOMEN Unlimited programs. While you can do a lot by yourself, you can do a lot more with others. Develop those relationships that inform you about the business, inform you about yourself, and keep you honest as you navigate your career.

3. DEVELOP PATIENCE
   AND AN EYE FOR OPPORTUNITY

   In times of challenge or crisis, it's difficult to see opportunity, but it's there. In every bad situation, there is an opportunity. When things happen that you can't change, such as the financial meltdown, ask yourself, "Okay, how can I make this work?"

4. KEEP ASSESSING AND LEARNING

   Avoid making a plan and sticking to the plan and blindly moving forward. Constantly evaluate what's working, why it's working, what you can learn, and how you can become a stronger leader.

Racioppi lives the advice she gives to emerging women leaders. Her own track record of deep and continual learning, patience, planning during her transition to the role of President and CEO, and collaboration with team members and corporate partners, speaks for itself. Female or male, we do well to learn from her example.

SUMMARY

1. Rosina Racioppi is President and CEO of WOMEN Unlimited, Inc., a world-renowned organization focusing on
   developing women leaders in major corporations. Because of its ability to pinpoint, develop, and retain diverse
   high-potential leadership talent, WOMEN Unlimited is
   the go-to development partner for over 160 leading organizations.

2. Racioppi took the helm at WOMEN Unlimited when the
   organization was 15 years old. To help with the transition,
   the leadership team expanded the board and also hired a
   coach to work with them around how they were evolving
   as an organization, how roles were changing, and how
   they needed to support one another. This process, involving open, transparent conversations, aligns with what
   WOMEN Unlimited teaches clients in their programs.

3. A distinguishing feature of WOMAN Unlimited is the ongoing frank conversations managers and facilitators hold
   with women and mentors in extended programs. These
   conversations reveal patterns, challenges, and concerns,
   as well as strategies women are employing in today's
   marketplace. Because of the breadth and depth of these
   conversations, WOMEN Unlimited can provide insights
   without breaking confidences or trust, a sacred commitment to partners. This information can provide a competitive edge in recruiting and retaining diverse talent.

4. WOMEN Unlimited reaches beyond the women enrolled
   in their programs. The conversations that are integral to
   the program allow for a genuine partnership with managers and mentors—including the men in the organization.
   In this way, WOMEN Unlimited is in a unique position to
   support an organization's desire to have women advancing in the organization.

5. Racioppi believes that to be effective in business, a team
   must have honest dialogue to address issues before they

become major challenges or obstacles. As she stepped into her new role, Racioppi worked to create pathways of communication within the team so that she could understand what was happening and assess alignment within the organization. She had to ensure the team members were communicating and sharing a common vision as the organization evolved.

6.   WOMEN Unlimited is committed to deep, strategic partnerships with clients. During the economic downturn of 2007 and 2008, many of the corporate partners were challenged, without budgets to participate in programs. WOMEN Unlimited worked with their partners to create workable strategies so that partners didn't lose ground during the crisis. This allowed partners to stay involved with WOMEN Unlimited until the budgets came back around. The organization took a hit, but because WOMEN Unlimited worked with the realities of their clients, they maintained all of their corporate partners.

7.   An effective CEO is mindful of her presence as the face of the organization. Racioppi believes that one role of an organization's top leader is to ensure the firm has the credentials and validation to do what it does. To maintain the organization's depth and credentials, Racioppi decided to pursue a doctorate in education, with support from her business partners, as a strategic initiative. Both the credential and the learning have strengthened the organization.

8.   When asked what advice she would give to young women just starting a career, Racioppi makes the following four suggestions: Develop the habit of curiosity; don't try to do it alone; develop patience and an eye for opportunity; and keep assessing and learning.

Your Notes and Reflections

_____

_____

_____

_____

_____

_____

_____

_____

_____

_____

_____

_____

_____

_____

_____

_____

CHAPTER 14

WHAT DOES IT
MEAN FOR YOU?

L eadership and pivotal moments go hand-in-
hand. For example, when an organization
is investigating a significant opportunity or seeking investors,
things become intense. The same is true when an organization
is up against a crisis stemming from economic changes, technology shifts, competitive challenges, or unforeseen factors.

When opportunities and challenges arise, leaders must
muster all their resources to address the associated challenges
and manage them well. They have to assess, plan, and act.
Otherwise, an opportunity that looks good can be a bust and a
crisis can cause a company to close its doors.

During intense and ambiguous times, people look to the
person who is at the helm of the ship, the captain. They look at
the CEO and the team of people who occupy executive leadership roles. They scrutinize the ways in which the leaders are
steering the ship forward in the face of ambiguity. After all,
their livelihoods, as well as their sense of purpose, are at stake.

You'll remember that Ron Ricci, co-author of *The Collaboration Imperative*, says that decisions are like best-selling
novels:

*The greater the ambiguity around a decision, the faster
it moves up the New York Times bestseller list. People's
natural curiosities and ambiguity seem to feed on each
other. In worst cases, ambiguity leads to conspiracy
theories and people work against each other. In most*

cases, work simply slows down while people seek out answers.

Ricci also says:

There's more than enough evidence to demonstrate that teams produce higher results when they can align their individual work to the greater mission and strategy of the organization. When all goes right, organizations can produce discretionary effort—that amazing, hard-to-bottle effort people give when ambiguity is replaced by a sense of shared purpose.

A leader's job is not only to get the business decisions right, but to inspire that discretionary effort that can make a company soar. As Nido Qubein says, leadership is about creating capacity in others.

The 12 executives who graciously shared their stories in the pages of this book serve as models of effective leadership—ones who create that essential discretionary effort. These executives represent personalities, industries, opportunities, and crises that run the global gamut. No matter your personality, industry, or circumstance, you can find a role model in these pages.

Perhaps more important, you now have access to a collection of 10 leadership behaviors to which these exemplary executives are committed. These 10 behaviors stretch beyond theories; they are behaviors that have been proven in the crucible of real organizations in some of the toughest business times and situations.

Chances are that you are more proficient in some of the leadership behaviors than others. That's okay, because, as we've seen in these pages, effective leaders constantly seek to grow and learn.

We encourage you to review the 10 leadership behaviors and commit to growing in each, one behavior at a time. Remember that the first five behaviors have to do with you—

with establishing the foundation you need to remain calm and clearheaded in the face of challenge or opportunity. You need a measure of fortitude and a network of support in place before major change or uncertainty strikes. The second five behaviors focus on your followers and other stakeholders. These are the communication behaviors that provide clarity and meaning in the face of uncertainty.

Think of these 10 behaviors as integrated, each building on the other, and you have a lifetime challenge to grow and improve. That's what a leader does. Here are the 10 leadership behaviors that lead to clarity and meaning:

1. ACCEPT THE REALITY THAT
    BUSINESS CYCLES INEVITABLY EBB AND FLOW
    Accepting rather than fighting this reality will help you to cultivate and communicate patience, perseverance, and confidence. These are essential components of leadership presence.

2. CULTIVATE THE HABITS OF LISTENING AND LEARNING
    Cutting-edge experts have recently begun promoting this behavior that came through so clearly in our interviews. In fact, Tomas Chamorro-Premuzic recently penned a blog post for the *Harvard Business Review* entitled, "Curiosity Is as Important as Intelligence." The hunger to grow and learn is essential to successfully negotiating complex situations.

3. CULTIVATE AUTHENTIC HUMILITY
    While it may seem difficult to balance humility with command and confidence, the best leaders do so. As you grow, be aware that there is much you can't know. Accept your limitations and seek out the strengths of others. This allows you to get the most complete information possible, and it allows others to develop and contribute meaningfully.

4. CLARIFY AND FOCUS ON THE
   ORGANIZATION'S MISSION AND VALUES
   The leader is the keeper of the organization's purpose.
   Without a shared purpose and values, employees won't
   have the loyalty, alignment, or energy the organization
   needs to succeed. Clarify your mission and repeat it often.
   It's not enough to post your organization's mission and
   values. It's your job to breathe life into them in practical
   ways. Frame all your communication to highlight these.

5. GET OUT OF THE WAY SO OTHERS CAN SUCCEED
   Think of yourself as the facilitator of others' work and
   growth, rather than the one in control. Emulate Sheila
   Jordan, who reviews her calendar every Sunday night to
   decide which things she can shed rather than try to control. This will help you develop leaders while getting the
   maximum impact with your own time.

6. BUILD A SOLID NETWORK OF RELATIONSHIPS
   Your success depends upon a network of relationships.
   Such networks provide knowledge, problem-solving advice, emotional support, mentorship, and more. Build a
   network both internal and external to your organization—
   and do it sooner rather than later. You are never so experienced that you can stop building your network.

7. BUILD STRATEGIC PARTNERSHIPS
   Boards of directors, customers, suppliers, and venture
   capitalists are all stakeholders who can be strategic partners contributing to your organization's success. Especially in times of crisis, these partnerships, if handled well,
   can make all the difference in the world. Actively cultivate partnerships in which every party wins.

8. CARE FOR AND REWARD YOUR PEOPLE
   People will always be your most important asset. Communicate this by listening to them, acknowledging their
   contributions, and rewarding them with pay and promotions.

9. Over communicate with all stakeholders, especially in times of crisis or change

Consistent communication is essential in every business climate, but in times of crisis, change, and uncertainty, it becomes even more important. Our participants spoke with conviction about the need for transparency, consistent messaging, and stepping up to tough conversations. Give frequent, honest feedback about performance, and support your people when they make mistakes.

10. Build trust and buy-in

Leaders who impose solutions do not foster the discretionary effort every organization needs. Leaders who create processes that allow others to create strategies and discover solutions do. Building trust and buy-in takes time, patience, effort, and a measure of humility. There is no shortcut and no room to arrogance.

Authors Jim Kouzes and Barry Posner of *Leadership Learning,* sum up what it means to be a leader, "Leadership is a choice. Either you chose to be one, or you don't. You have options in life. But when you make the choice, you are taking responsibility for that action."

The responsibility that comes with leadership will never be easy, but it can be intensely rewarding. The need to learn, grow, and deeply listen to others will never end, but neither will the richness that comes with personal and organizational growth. It's with a tremendous sense of satisfaction that you can say, "I helped others grow and become leaders; I developed capacity in others."

Of course, everything starts with growing capacity in yourself. You know 10 leadership communication behaviors that will change how you and those who follow you will see the world and perform. Grow into those behaviors, one behavior at a time.

It's time to begin!

ASH SEDDEEK AND LESLIE A. RUBIN
Founders
Executive Greatness Institute

Ash and Leslie are founders of the Executive Greatness Institute (EGI). EGI is a leadership communication company offering services to help business leaders create a strong leadership brand, executive presence, and develop a solid messaging platform. They pride themselves on helping leaders hone their communications skills by working with a dream team of executive coaches and experts.

Having extensive experience working with C-level executives both inside corporations and as outside consultants, Ash and Leslie have the skills to analyze and craft messages that lead to recognizable brands and business growth.

You can count on them to understand your leadership communication challenges. They work with leaders one on one to help them accelerate personal leadership capability or work with their teams on larger communication and leadership development efforts.

Learn more at:

Website .... : http://www.ExecutiveGreatness.com

Email .... : info@ExecutiveGreatness.com

Ash .... : 916-753-7432

Leslie .... : 650-255-8839

CHAPTER 15

ABOUT THE AUTHORS

ASH SEDDEEK is a best-selling author and a profit maximization and leadership coach. He uncovered the success secrets of the top 1 percent of entrepreneurs and sales professionals and combines these secrets with his Own It Win It Crush It™ Profit Success Formula. Ash helps businesses, entrepreneurs, and sellers to accelerate their transformation and profits so they can pursue their bigger purpose and have the impact they are looking for on the world at large.

Website ..... : http://www.ExecutiveGreatness.com

Email .... : Ash@ConnectWithAsh.com

LESLIE A. RUBIN is CEO of Image Matterz Consulting, a global executive, and strategic communications consultancy focused on helping leaders develop their business communications skills and executive brand. Regarded as an expert in executive communications, Leslie has worked with C-suite business leaders at Cisco Systems, Oracle Corporation and SAP.

Website ..... : http://ImageMatterzConsulting.com

Email .... : Leslie@ImageMatterzConsulting.com